PENGUIN BO

The Wanderer

Michael Alexander's verse translations from Old English include *The Earliest English Poems* (1966) and *Beowulf* (1973), both in Penguin Classics, and *Old English Riddles from the Exeter Book* (Anvil Press, 1980, 2007, 2013). Other publications are Penguin editions of *Beowulf* and of Chaucer, a study of Ezra Pound, and a well-liked *History of English Literature* (Palgrave, 2000, 2007). He has retired from the Chair of English Literature at the University of St Andrews and now lives in Oxford. His most recent publications are *Medievalism: The Middle Ages in Modern England* (Yale University Press, 2007), *The First Poems in English* (Penguin, 2008) and *Reading Shakespeare* (Palgrave, 2012).

The Wanderer

Elegies, Epics, Riddles

Translated and Edited by MICHAEL ALEXANDER

PENGUIN BOOKS

PENGUIN CLASSICS

Published by the Penguin Group
Penguin Books Ltd, 80 Strand, London WC2R ORL, England
Penguin Group (USA) Inc., 375 Hudson Street, New York, New York 10014, USA
Penguin Group (Canada), 90 Eglinton Avenue East, Suite 700, Toronto, Ontario, Canada M4P 2Y3 (a
division of Pearson Penguin Canada Inc.)
Penguin Ireland, 25 St Stephen's Green, Dublin 2, Ireland (a division of Penguin Books Ltd)
Penguin Group (Australia), 707 Collins Street, Melbourne, Victoria 3008, Australia
(a division of Pearson Australia Group Pty Ltd)
Penguin Books India Pvt Ltd, 11 Community Centre, Panchsheel Park, New Delhi – 110 017, India
Penguin Group (NZ), 67 Apollo Drive, Rosedale, Auckland 0632, New Zealand
(a division of Pearson New Zealand Ltd)
Penguin Books (South Africa) (Pty) Ltd, Block D, Rosebank Office Park, 181 Jan Smuts Avenue,
Parktown North, Gauteng 2193, South Africa

Penguin Books Ltd, Registered Offices: 80 Strand, London WC2R ORL, England

www.penguin.com

Translation first published 1966; revised and expanded 1991
This edition first published in Penguin Classics 2008
Reissued in Penguin Classics 2013
001

TO
EZRA POUND

CONTENTS

———— z ————

INTRODUCTION

———— z ————

In the gloom the gold gathers the light against it

THE excuse, ultimately, for a book of this sort is a conviction on the part of the author that some early English poems deserve to be read by those who do not make their living out of the subject, that what is excellent should be made current. Not much Old English verse has survived, but among the debris there are some very fine things, finer perhaps and more numerous than anything which has survived of the poetry of any continental Germanic people. I have tried to translate only the very best of them.

Anglo-Saxon will never be considered one of the great literatures of the world. This fact, obvious to those who do not know the language, has sometimes escaped those who do. Few Anglo-Saxon scholars seem to have been qualified to evaluate the poems, and, indeed, very few have even tried to carry out this primary critical duty, though W. P. Ker was a notable exception. On the other hand, the achievements of Anglo-Saxon England in the arts have generally been forgotten or undervalued by those who have no professional interest in them, the main reason being the scarcity of evidence. All that we have of the verse is four manuscript books – four very miscellaneous collections – and there is no means of knowing whether all the principal kinds of Old English composition are represented in them. There is no reason to suppose, either, that what Time has spared is necessarily the best. Again, the texts may have been copied out many times before they found their way into these books, and it is impossible, in our present state of ignorance, to gauge what relationship text bears to original composition, probably oral. Did the poet dictate to a monk scribe? Could he himself write? We cannot tell. In short, we know very little, and every new discovery emphasizes the extent of our ignorance. For instance the finding, in 1939, of a ship-burial at Sutton Hoo in Suffolk necessitated a revision of several of our assumptions about the religion, art, trade and wealth of the Anglo-Saxons.

Our ignorance is what makes the ages that elapsed between the end of the Roman Empire and the beginnings of Provençal song so very dark for the recorder of poetic achievement. So little has survived 'the martyrdom of jakes and fire'; and, in the case of the Old English verse that we have, the language has since changed so much that it is hardly recognizable as English. This means that we have had to call in Philology as midwife to the Muse; but, with honourable exceptions, the keepers of the word-hoard have acted more as dragons than as modest *ancillae*. And the dustiness of literary historians of this period has led less docile students to suppose of our earliest poems what cannot be supposed of any poem – that they are exclusively 'of academic interest'.

Besides the insufficiency of the evidence, and its inaccessibility, there is another reason for the neglect of Old English poetry and Northern literature in general: the fact that nearly all our ideas of religion and art have come from the Mediterranean, that Italy has been the matrix and France the mediatrix of our civilization. We are still heirs to the prejudices of the Renaissance, though certainly in an attenuated form; at least, they serve us as an excuse not to study the Middle Ages. But anyone who reads, say, *The Ruin*, *The Seafarer*, *The Dream of the Rood* and *The Battle of Maldon* – less than six hundred lines in all – will discard (if he ever had it) any idea that between the fall of Rome and the revival of learning Europe was a battleground where ignorant German armies clashed by night, and that the darkness of the age was deliberately maintained by Benedictine monks.

Alexander Pope included in the *Dunciad* one Thomas Hearne, who printed the first edition of *The Battle of Maldon*. 'But who is he,' he asks,

in closet close ypent,
Of sober face, with learned dust besprent?
Right well mine eyes arede the myster wight
On parchment scraps yfed, and Wurmius hight.
To future ages may thy dulness last,
As thou preserv'st the dulness of the past!

In fact, this particular piece of dullness by our 'rude forefathers' was nearer to Homer's oral *poiesis* than his English translator knew.

The mention of the *Iliad*, of course, puts *Maldon* in its place: nothing in Anglo-Saxon verse has the range or stature of Homer. But, at its best, the early English verse was highly accomplished, formally eloquent, charged with a sober intensity: it has epic qualities. Far from being crude or barbarous, its technique was fully developed, and *Beowulf* might almost be called baroque in style. The alliterative fashion of poetry came into England on the crest of an inestimably ancient oral tradition, whose credentials were those of Homer himself.

Despite the thousand years that separate us from the old poets, and despite the changes which make them seem so remote, it is worth the labour of acquainting ourselves with their archaic but durable verses. Reading them, we ascend to the source of the English language, where words are rooted in things and full of meaning – perhaps more fully meant. Our predecessors in these islands lived simpler, less comfortable, less 'civilized' lives; but it does not seem to have done their poetry any harm.

II

An Angle or a Saxon (or a Jute) was of Germanic stock; and Anglo-Saxon, or Old English – the language of England for seven centuries – belongs to the Germanic group of languages. West Germanic is a branch of Indo-European and, like Greek and Latin, it is an inflected language: the endings indicate the function of the word, and word-order is variable. However, Old English prose never achieved the sophisticated word-order or complex syntax of Greek or Latin.

This does not apply to the verse. Poetry seems an older human accomplishment than prose, and the poets used a special archaic diction inherited from days when their art had been purely oral. This word-hoard amounts almost to a language within a language: it differs greatly in vocabulary and syntax from the rudimentary attempts of the prose-writers – because, as I have said, Anglo-Saxon poetry belongs to an oral tradition as old as the Germanic tribes themselves.

In such a society the poet is the keeper of the traditions which hold the *cynn* (kin) together, just as the king (*cyn-ing*) is the keeper of the treasure which is the *cynn*'s only possession and defence. The older a sword was, the older a word was, the more it was valued by the *cynn*. In a primitive society the poet is historian and priest, and his songs have ritual significance. That is why the language of the poets was so deeply conservative, and why the written records of it that we have show it so different from the language of the earliest prose-writers.

III

In *Beowulf*, when the warriors are riding back from the mere where the monster, Grendel, has died from the mortal wound Beowulf inflicted on him, they talk of the great feat which has liberated them. To shorten the journey, they run races, or

> a fellow of the king's
> whose head was a storehouse of the storied verse,
> whose tongue gave gold to the language
> of the treasured repertory, wrought a new lay
> made in the measure.
> > The man struck up,
> found the phrase, framed rightly
> the deed of Beowulf, drove the tale,
> rang word-changes. He chose to speak
> first of Sigemund, sang the most part
> of what he had heard of that hero's exploits.

This passage is, perhaps more than any other, a key to the

understanding of the old poetry. It illustrates clearly many important points: it shows that extempore oral composition on a recent event was a normal thing, and that the audience evidently delighted in technical accomplishment; it also gives us some clues as to what they considered the finer points of that accomplishment. Most interesting of all, it shows us the birth of a legend. Beowulf had boasted that he would kill the monster, and did so: word becomes deed. In gratitude, the people he has delivered honour him in a lay: deed becomes word.

The poet compares him first with Sigemund, the greatest of all the dragon-slayers of Germanic tradition. The process of lay-making is here presented as normal – and it is still a regular activity among unlettered peoples even today. But there is no extant lay of Sigemund in English, despite the fact that the audience of *Beowulf* are obviously expected to know who he is. The heroic poems *Widsith* and *Deor* also allude to stories which were presumably already well known to the audience. In the centuries of Anglo-Saxon literacy these lays must have been written down. Of the 'treasured repertory', what remains? What is left of the word-hoard?

IV

In the catalogue of the donations of Leofric, first bishop of Exeter, to the library of Exeter Cathedral, there is *i mycel englisc boc be gehwilcum thingum on leothwisan geworht* – one big English book about every sort of thing, wrought in song-wise. This is the 'Exeter Book', the chief of the four codices of Old English poetry.

Exeter, like Worcester and the other cathedrals of the West Country, escaped the Danish raids, and the *mycel englisc boc* has survived the vicissitudes of a thousand years. (Though not unscathed: the front has been used as a cutting-board and, more appropriately, as a beer mat; the back fourteen pages have been burnt through by a brand.)

The miscellaneous contents of the Exeter Book are half on

Christian, half on secular themes. The scribes were monks: and the bulk of the thirty thousand or so lines of Old English poetry that remain is Christian. Of the three other collections of the poetry now extant, two – those in the Bodleian Library and in the library of Vercelli Cathedral – are given over entirely to dramatic paraphrases of Old Testament stories or of saints' lives. The other book (the Cotton MS in the British Museum) contains *Beowulf*, but most of the rest of it is devoted to works of edification, some of them in prose.

So: there are thirty thousand lines left, mostly on Christian themes. I have translated only one of the Christian poems; and have attempted only four passages from *Beowulf*, the most famous Anglo-Saxon poem. Why so?

The Christian poems – especially *Genesis*, *Exodus* and *Judith* – have some very fine things in them. But, broadly speaking, the old poets were happiest when dealing with themes of the Germanic past, and, apart from *The Dream of the Rood*, there is no one Anglo-Saxon poem that can be said to have fully assimilated themes of Latin provenance. In this belief I have chosen to translate what I consider the authentic, autochthonous Anglo-Saxon poems; not from any prejudice against Christianity – far from it – nor from a love of the septentrional savage, but because these poems – the 'elegies' and *The Battle of Maldon* – seem to me the best.

'*Beowulf*, because it is extant, has sometimes been overvalued, as if it were the work of an English Homer. But it was not preserved, as the *Iliad* was, by the unanimous judgement of all the people through successive generations.' In this remark W. P. Ker shows the balance and sense which distinguished him from other historians of the literature of the dark ages, and make his *Mediaeval English Literature* still the best general introduction. However, *Beowulf*, as he says, is the 'best worth studying' of the Anglo-Saxon poems: because, being the longest surviving heroic poem, it gives us the completest picture of the heroic world, and also because it works up to passages of epic magnificence – some of which I have attempted. But *Beowulf* has stolen the attention of editors (and hence of students) from the poems I have translated here; in them, I believe, the *virtù* of Old English is to be found in its purest and most concentrated form.

V

Before introducing the individual poems, I must briefly list some of the chief changes that have taken place in the function and style of poetry in the thousand years since the poems were written down, and which necessarily condition our attitude to them.

First, changes in the structure of society have completely altered the role of the poet. In a millennium, English society, from being a collection of close-knit clans or *cynns*, each loyal to its lord, has become huge, centralized, and with functions so differentiated that 'the centre cannot hold' and the community has, for all except practical purposes, disintegrated. Its members have few common interests and there is no *communis sententia*, no common sense. Consequently no poet can speak for the community.

The Old English poet up until Alfred's time was a man with a public function: he was the voice and memory of the tribe. When the lord called upon him for a lay, everyone in the hall listened: through him the tradition was made new, the common fund of experience was brought to bear on the present. Knowing the past, he could interpret life as it came, making it part of the tale of the tribe. *The Battle of Maldon*, for example, is a record of a battle fought against the Danes in 991; it is a more sober and reliable account than is to be found in later Latin historians, and it must have been accepted as the true story by anyone who heard it. So the verdict of Tacitus – that 'these ancient songs are the only sort of history or annals that they possess' – holds good of the Anglo-Saxons eight hundred years after it was written about their ancestors, the illiterate inhabitants of Germania. The battle is also recorded (twice) in the annals of the Anglo-Saxon Chronicle; but poetry, with the Chronicle, the laws, and the archaeological evidence, is still the chief source of early English history.

How different is the position of the poet today! From being an interpreter of life to his *cynn* – an acknowledged legislator – he has been relegated to the fringe of a literate, half-educated society. If verse is read today outside schools it is often in the context of

> A shaded lamp and a waving blind
> And the beat of a clock from a distant floor

– it is a private, silent affair. Anything less like the art of public oral composition from which Anglo-Saxon literature developed, and to which, at its most characteristic, it approximates, is not easily imagined.

Secondly, the style of poetry has changed from an oral to a literary mode. 'Oral literature' is a contradiction in terms, and the conventions of composition on paper differ radically from those of unrehearsed composition in public. It is true that the only records we have of the old poems are, in the nature of the case, written, which means that they were either dictated by the poet to a scribe or written down by the poet himself. According to the pioneers of research into living oral epic – Milman Parry and Albert B. Lord – the process of writing down an orally composed poem inhibits the characteristic oral style, slowing it down so that the run of the rhythm is lost. But the Old English poems show all the characteristics of this oral style enumerated by Lord in his fascinating book, *The Singer of Tales*. Are we to think that all these poems were dictated? Could none of the poets have been able to write? Though I respect Lord's view that it is misleading to speak of a 'transitional' style between oral and literary, I think that in this detail of his thesis he is being too schematic. Though the two modes of composition are certainly different in kind, they can appear in the same work in a way that may justly be called mixed or even transitional.

What are the characteristics of an oral style? They arise from the necessity of not breaking down during performance. In order to keep the self-imposed 'rules' of Anglo-Saxon metric the *scop*, or poet,★ had always to have a formula ready, an instinctive reflex to the metrical necessities of rapid composition. For it must not be thought that the oral poets memorized their lays; of course they had the main outline of the story by heart, but any theme or episode could be embroidered, contracted, changed or dropped altogether, according to the receptivity of the audience on that particular evening. New themes might be borrowed from another lay, or a flattering reference to the ancestors of the lord before whom the lay was being sung might be introduced (it is fairly obvious that this happened in *Beowulf* and in *Widsith*). Every re-telling was a new poem, each as authentic, original and authoritative as the last; and every performance was different.

Once the minstrel had embarked on a lay, he was not expected to falter. The poets therefore learned a special sort of improvisation-aid, a poetic grammar or rhetoric which acted as scaffolding for their song, infinitely flexible, extensible, adaptable to the job in hand. To give an accurate idea of what was involved, an outline of Anglo-Saxon metric is necessary at this point.

Anglo-Saxon is a stressed language, and the metre of the verse is based on stresses and their relative weight; the number and length of syllables matter less. Pitch also played a part in the metric, as the poets show themselves composing to the harp; syllables counting as 'long' in modern versification are not necessarily stressed.

English is still a stressed language today, but Chaucer and Spenser and subsequent English versifiers imitated the French, Italian, Latin and Greek practice of counting syllables. We called our unstressed syllable short and our stressed syllable long, and adopted feet and pentameters and all the

---

★ *Scop* is related to the preterite of *scieppan*, 'to shape, form, create, destine', and to *scieppend*, 'creator, shaper, God'. It is thus the exact equivalent of 'poet', which is similarly related to ποιεῖν, 'to make'; and of *makar*, the old Scots word for poet. Provençal *trobator*, North French *trouvère* and Italian *trovatore*, on the other hand, come from a 'find' root, indicating more modest aspirations.

terminology of quantitative versification. Rhymed or unrhymed, the accentual iambic pentameter held the field until the beginning of this century, until the mould was broken by Pound and Eliot and a new start made. But traditional versification has many stout adherents; the sound of

> So all day long the noise of battle roll'd

still preconditions the ear of the reader.

By contrast, the number of syllables in an Anglo-Saxon line may vary between eight and about twenty. But there are normally four main stresses, two on either side of a distinct break in the middle of the line. For example:

> || Or a *fel*low of the *king's*
> whose *head* was a *store*house || of the *storied verse,*
> whose *tongue gave* || *gold* to the *lang*uage
> of the *treasured repertory,* || *wrought* a *new* lay
> *made* in the *measure.* || The *man struck* up,
> *found* the *phrase,* || *framed right*ly
> the *deed* of *Beow*ulf.||

Formulaic characteristics suggest that the italicized syllables were stressed in recitation, and the mid-line pause may have been marked by a stroke of the harp. It is this mid-line pause which organizes the line. Sentences usually begin after it, and the key of the alliteration is the initial letter of the first stress in the second half-line. One of the stresses in the first half-line must alliterate with it, and the other may. The last stress of the line must not alliterate.

Thus, loosely:

> *O*ne or *o*ther of the *o*pening *s*tresses
> *M*ust al*l*iterate with the *l*eading *s*yllable
> In the *s*econd *h*alf-line; *s*ometimes *b*oth do,
> In *t*riple *fr*ont-rhyme; the *f*ourth is *d*ifferent.

The number of unstressed syllables is variable; in the strictest verse (e.g. in *Beowulf*) they are kept to a minimum, but towards the end of the period – in *Maldon*, for example – the number of unimportant syllables slackens the tension of the line.

Anyone who will speak aloud, or, better, declaim vigorously the lines quoted above, will soon get by ear the characteristic Anglo-Saxon rhythm. It is a formalized version of the rhythm of emphatic speech, derived originally from the rhythm of the heart and the rhythm of the breath. The placings of the weak syllables among the heavy stresses may give five types of half-line, as set out in Appendix C. But the ear soon gets a grasp of the 'permissible' moulds.

In learning the possible forms of the half-line, the reader is going through the same process as does the apprentice singer. The half-line – a verbal and musical phrase containing two stresses – is the basic unit of Old English metric, and the singer would pause before and after each half-line. The halves are bound together over the mid-line break by an alliterative brace, but the important consideration in this kind of verse is the rhythm, the distribution of the stresses – not the alliteration, as is often thought.

The end of the line – so important in rhymed, end-stopped, or stanzaic verse, or any sort of printed poetry – is the creation of the editors of the Old English poems, for in the original MSS the poems are written as continuous prose, the quill stopping at the edge of the page. The end of the line, indeed, is far less important than in rhymed verse, the last stress actually breaking the alliteration instead of repeating it.

Once the apprentice singer has learnt to 'think in half-lines', he must learn the art of construction – of binding half-lines into sentences, sentences into episodes, and episodes into stories. All the time that he sings out his unfaltering series of half-lines, the poet must not lose sight of the direction of the story. And it must not be thought that an oral poem is necessarily an uncomplicated one. *Beowulf* was not sung in one evening; and Milman Parry tape-recorded a lay sung by Avdo Methedović of Yugoslavia which ran to 12,000 lines – as long as one of the Homeric poems.

Analysing these long poems, Parry proved that Homer depended on his ability to produce, for every idea, a formula. He defined the 'formula' as: 'a group of words which is regularly employed under the same metrical conditions to express a given essential idea'. The application of Parry's systematic analysis to Anglo-Saxon* has shown that, for example, of the first fifty half-lines in *Beowulf* only thirteen are not matched wholly or in part elsewhere in Anglo-Saxon verse – in part, because minor adaptations of the formula can take place. Professor Magoun instanced the Old English phrase for 'a long time ago' or 'in the past': this could be *gear-dagum*, *aer-dagum*, or *eald-dagum* according to the exigencies of the alliterative pattern. Likewise, the idea 'for a long time' could be rendered by *ealle hwile*, *lange hwile*, or *micele hwile*; or, if it suited the alliteration, by *ealle thrage*, *lange thrage*, or *micele thrage*. It is probable that if the corpus of Old English verse were larger, nearly every half-line could be paralleled elsewhere.

By building up this vocabulary of phrases and developing the knack of stringing them together into 'runs' – to the point where it has become instinctive – the oral poet achieves mastery of his art. It is at this stage, when he begins to compose with and through the form rather than simply *in* it, that the poet can begin to use his material. Paradoxically, as the material of Anglo-Saxon and most oral poetry is traditional, it is truer to say that it is precisely when the *scop* has learned to use the language that the tradition is tapped, and can begin to use him as its anonymous vehicle. At this milestone the convenient distinction between form and material has to be discarded, because 'the tradition' does not exist apart from the language – it is inherent in its idioms and rhythms. In any great passage of verse – as, say, Prospero's 'cloud-capped palaces' speech, or 'the Lay of the Last Survivor' in *Beowulf* – the poet becomes invisible. The polarity employed by modern criticism between tradition and originality has a limited usefulness in this context. One has the distinct impression that the 'shaping spirit' has put the whole machinery of composition into overdrive.

* By F. P. Magoun Jr, in *Speculum*, Vol. 28, 1953.

At such moments the correlation of the forces controlling the artist is, as it were, stood on its head. The ascendancy is no longer with the artist or the state of mind which he is trying to express, but with the language, his instrument of expression. Language, the home and dwelling of beauty and meaning, itself begins to think and speak for man and turns wholly into music, not in the sense of outward, audible sounds but by virtue of the power and momentum of its inward flow. Then, like the current of a mighty river polishing stones and turning wheels by its very movement, the flow of speech creates in passing, by the force of its own laws, rhyme and rhythm and countless other forms and formations, still more important and until now undiscovered, unconsidered and unnamed.*

There are many parallel and synonymous formulas for the commonest ideas in early English verse – for man, God, sea, lord, joy, battle, death, exile, and grief. In one way, these alternatives acted, metrically, as stopgaps for the poet, giving him time to think of the second half of the line while he automatically sang a phrase reinforcing the meaning of, say, the first half of the previous line. This parallelism and the resulting variation slow down the movement of the verse, lending it dignity and solidity and a highly-wrought, formal texture. Some of the traditional figures are richly metaphoric: the sun is frequently *woruld-candel*, the sea is *swan-rad* – 'swan's riding'. (This sort of double-barrelled metaphor is called a *kenning*.) All language is, of course, metaphoric in origin (we can only speak of what we do not know in terms of what we know), but Anglo-Saxon has a metaphoric density to which no modern translation can do justice.

Finally, I must re-emphasize that if Old English verse is rich and formal, it inherits these qualities from ritual language. The vocabulary and the technique of oral composition come down from times when poetry was mantic and used for magical purposes, when it played an inseparable part in the rituals that introduced, celebrated, and interpreted the events and seasons of men's lifetimes and of the natural year.

---

* *Doctor Zhivago*, Chapter XIV, Section 8.

This sacred and magical quality good poetry has never altogether lost, but as, down the ages, religion and poetry have become separate, tradition in the arts has often hardened into convention, and convention has produced, by reaction, the desire to be different. The thirst for originality has no part in oral poetry, though no lay was ever sung the same way twice; conversely, plagiarism was impossible in oral verse. As Parry says, 'one oral poet is better than another not because he has by himself found a more striking way of expressing his thought, but because he has been better able to make use of the tradition'.

A NOTE ON THE TRANSLATION

———*z*———

I HAVE never seen the point of translating verse into anything but verse. 'The other harmony of prose' may be useful for a first impression, or for 'the story' of a narrative poem; and it may be that any translation is better than none. But it seems to me that the first aim in translating a living poem from a language which happens to be unknown into one's own language is to produce something with art in it, something which lives. I do not mean that there is no art of prose; but dictionary meanings strung together into 'prose' give 'what was said', with no idea of the way it was said.★ All the poetry, it seems to me, is in the way it was said, and it is in this belief that I have borrowed the form of the Old English verse in making these versions.

I am aware that reproducing the metre and keeping to the 'rules' of the original do not necessarily deliver the goods. But in Anglo-Saxon verse the form is of the essence. For one thing, as Ezra Pound remarked, it is our *only* indigenous form. But above all, it is a form which reinforces the meaning: the stresses fall on the four most important words in the line and the alliteration binds the fabric of the meaning together. The frequent parallelisms re-state and re-embody the meaning; and, most important of all, the assonance (embracing both consonance and dissonance) of the four stressed words of one line with the four stressed words of the preceding and succeeding lines gives Old English verse a unique robustness,

---

★ Since writing the above I came across this sentence in Fenollosa's *The Chinese Written Character as a Medium for Poetry*: 'Sinologues should remember that the purpose of poetical translation is the poetry not the verbal definitions in dictionaries.'

resonance, and force. The valorousness of the sound is intransmissible, but it seemed an effect worth striving after.

My aim, therefore, has been to keep to the original metre as far as possible and at all times to give a faithful impression of its vigour. I have been more careful to achieve a correct stress-pattern than to keep the alliteration absolutely regular. Local departures from the strict classical form have been made for reasons that seemed to me good at the time.

The diction of the poems was traditional and archaic even at the time they were written down. It is probably true, as Richmond Lattimore says in introducing his *Iliad*, that there is no traditional poetic vocabulary left which is still usable. But in translating Old into Modern English, it seems uneconomic not to take advantage of the many words which have survived virtually unchanged. When I began to translate *The Ruin* five years ago I was fired by the example of Ezra Pound's version of *The Seafarer* (which gives far and away the most concentrated impression of Anglo-Saxon poetry); but half a century has elapsed since that *Seafarer*, and I have discovered, in extending Pound's translation method to all the best Old English poems, that certain archaisms (the *-eth* form, for example) are no longer generally practicable. So the last poems I have translated are noticeably less archaic in style than the first. But I hope that the principle upon which I decided not to exclude ancient or half-forgotten words if they could still be made to do their job still holds: it is that an old word tensed and tuned in a strict form, can still be made to yield its *virtù*.

In the art of the Anglo-Saxon *scop* the strong and durable frame of the traditional form sustained the vocabulary; in its intricately wrought setting an ancient word shone out like the stones on the Rood's crossbeam. The 'reclamation' policy of William Morris is no longer possible, but I still believe, despite J. R. R. Tolkien's condemnation of 'the etymological fallacy', that the life of a word comes from its root, and that the occasional use of a word in its original sense is one of the duties as well as the prerogatives of a poet. One has to risk making mistakes.

I have, then, retained as much of the metre and the traditional vocabulary of Anglo-Saxon poetry as was feasible, and in order to make this effort worth while, I must further strain the sympathy of the reader by asking him to read these translations *aloud*, and with as much vigour and deliberation as he finds the line warrants. I must also beg him to observe the mid-line pause, *without which the metric is incomprehensible*, and to pitch into the stresses. Such instructions, I am aware, are more proper to music than to poetry; and the poet cannot expect the reader to do his work for him. But Old English poetry was oral, therefore, aural; and if the reader can with the aid of the poems here translated, imagine a *scop*, a harp, and the hall hushed, he will be more than half-way there.

I have used some key Old English words 'neat' where I could find no modern equivalent. Apart from *cynn* and *scop*, already explained, the most important of them are:

    aetheling: son of some *aethel* or noble man, often a royal prince.

    burg: a fortified city, root of modern 'borough'.

    byrnie: a coat of mail.

    Hwaet: an exclamation made at the beginning of a poem or speech to call for attention, possibly accompanied by a chord on the harp.

    weard: 'ward', 'protector'; see *hlaf-weard*, p. 40

    wierd: this all-important word is related to *weorthan*, to be, become or happen. It means 'what is, what happens, the way that things happen. Fate, personal destiny, death'. Shakespeare's 'weird sisters', descended from the 'fatal sustren thre', the Norns of Norse mythology and the Parcae of Greek, have inherited some of the original force of the word. I spell it 'Wierd' or 'wierd' to distinguish it from the weaker modern adjective.

Anglo-Saxon pronunciation differed considerably from ours, but for the purposes of this book it will suffice to note that the '*c*' in which many proper names end was pronounced 'ch', as in 'church'; that the '*æ*' diphthong, also common in names, was pronounced as in 'flat hat'; and that '*sc*' was pronounced 'sh'. Every vowel is given its full value, so that Dunnere in *The Battle of Maldon*, for example, is a three-syllable rather than a two-syllable word.

Finally, I must warn students that all line references are to the Anglo-Saxon texts.

PREFACE TO THE SECOND
EDITION

————*z*————

IN twelve years some of the inaccuracies and omissions of the first edition have become obvious, and I am grateful for this chance to make corrections, though I have not attempted to cover my undergraduate tracks. Bibliographical suggestions have been brought up to date. The endings of *The Seafarer* and *The Dream of the Rood* have now been included, at a reader's request. Other shortcomings of the translations, introductions and notes have become clear, but I have not sought to put a wiser face on early enthusiasms. A fifth passage from *Beowulf* is added, taken from my more recent attempt, a translation different in style from *The Wife's Complaint*, just as that version differs in style from *The Ruin*, translated in 1959. These changes in style have made it difficult to change the translations. If the introductions were to be written today, they too would be different – I have grown to admire *Beowulf* deeply, and to sympathize with Latin Christian literates.

The first edition acknowledged all conscious debts, notably to the University of Oxford and some of its graduates. In preparing a second edition I should again like to offer my thanks to Mrs Radice for her editorial care, and, for lending her excellent ear, to my wife Eileen.

January, 1977 M.J.A.

PREFACE TO THE THIRD EDITION

———— z ————

IN preparing a third edition in 1990 of a volume commissioned by E. V. Rieu in 1960, I would like to record my gratitude to his successor Betty Radice, who persuaded me to translate *Beowulf*, and accepted Peter Whigham's *Poems of Catullus* and Arthur Cooper's *Li Po and Tu Fu* as Penguin Classics.

The study of Old English is no longer a part of most degrees in English literature, and the role of translation is the greater – both for prose cribs and for poetic versions like my own. There are now fewer Old English scholars, but more attractive introductions to Anglo-Saxon England, such as James Campbell's *The Anglo-Saxons*. Our enlarged understanding of the Latin background of Anglo-Saxon literacy is reflected in the revised suggestions for Further Reading.

I have not changed the text of the second edition very much. But I have added original texts of *Caedmon's Hymn* and *Bede's Death Song*, with translations, and have also added new translations of *Brunanburh* and a passage from *The Phoenix*, and nine further Riddles.

At the opening of a conference on the medieval and renaissance literature of Scotland held in 1981 at the University of Stirling the news was received that the Conservative government, led by a former Minister of Education, had cut the grant to universities by one tenth. Stirling had to cut its intake of students by one quarter. Mrs Joyce Dunn, the wife of Professor T. A. Dunn, pleased me that evening by quoting *Thaes ofereode, thisses swa maeg* – the refrain of the Old English poem known as *Deor*. I would like to dedicate this edition to that flourishing Department of English Studies.

St Andrews, 1990   M.J.A.

This is the sense but not the order of the words as he sang them in his sleep; for verses, though never so well composed, cannot be literally translated out of one language into another without loss of their beauty and loftiness.

Bede, of Caedmon's hymn.

. . . tha ongan ic ongemang othrum mislicum and manigfealdum bisgum thisses kynerices tha boc wendan on Englisc . . . hwilum word be worde, hwilum andgit of angiete . . .

Alfred, of Gregory's Cura Pastoralis.

THE RUIN

———z———

THIS description of a deserted Roman city, written on two leaves badly scarred by fire, may well stand at the gate of a selection of Anglo-Saxon poems. The Romans had held this province for four centuries before the Angles came; and they had been gone three centuries when this poem was written. It was to be another three hundred years before the Normans reintroduced the art of massive construction in stone to these islands. The Anglo-Saxons usually referred to Roman ruins as 'the work of the Giants'.

It is probable that the city of the poem is Aquae Sulis, the Roman Bath, and we may imagine the anonymous author walking about the overgrown streets. His thoughts as he does so are very like those of *The Wanderer* and the 'Last Survivor', and *The Ruin* is thought of as an Elegy. But, as Elliot van Kirk Dobbie remarks in his Introduction to *The Anglo-Saxon Poetic Records*, vol. III, 'the internal rimes, together with the unusual concreteness of the vocabulary, and the use of words elsewhere unrecorded in Anglo-Saxon set this poem quite apart from the other lyric-elegiac texts in The Exeter Book'. If we wish to tie in this unique poem to the corpus of Anglo-Saxon literature, we may think of it as the first of many English meditations on old stones. It compares interestingly with Gray's ponderings upon the 'rude forefathers' of Stoke Poges.

A less naturalistic and archaeological perspective for the poem has more recently been proposed: the ruined cities and empires foreseen in the Apocalypse and Augustine's *City of God*. The waters of such a Babylon may have found an echo in the imagination of a visitor to Bath.

I

The Ruin

Well-wrought this wall: Wierds broke it.
The stronghold burst . . . .

Snapped rooftrees, towers fallen,
the work of the Giants, the stonesmiths,
mouldereth.
                    Rime scoureth gatetowers
                    rime on mortar.

Shattered the showershields, roofs ruined,
age under-ate them.
                    And the wielders and wrights?
Earthgrip holds them – gone, long gone,
fast in gravesgrasp while fifty fathers
and sons have passed.
                    Wall stood,
grey lichen, red stone, kings fell often,
stood under storms, high arch crashed –
stands yet the wallstone, hacked by weapons,
by files grim-ground . . .
. . . shone the old skilled work
. . . sank to loam-crust.

Mood quickened mind, and a man of wit,
cunning in rings, bound bravely the wallbase
with iron, a wonder.

Bright were the buildings, halls where springs ran,
high, horngabled, much throng-noise;
these many mead-halls men filled
with loud cheerfulness: Wierd changed that.

Came days of pestilence, on all sides men fell dead,
death fetched off the flower of the people;
where they stood to fight, waste places
and on the acropolis, ruins.
                    Hosts who would build again

shrank to the earth. Therefore are these courts dreary
and that red arch twisteth tiles,
wryeth from roof-ridge, reacheth groundwards. . . .
Broken blocks. . . .

      There once many a man
mood-glad, goldbright, of gleams garnished,
flushed with wine-pride, flashing war-gear,
gazed on wrought gemstones, on gold, on silver,
on wealth held and hoarded, on light-filled amber,
on this bright burg of broad dominion.

Stood stone houses; wide streams welled
hot from source, and a wall all caught
in its bright bosom, that the baths were
hot at hall's hearth; that was fitting . . .
. . . .

Thence hot streams, loosed, ran over hoar stone
unto the ring-tank . . . .
  . . . It is a kingly thing
  . . . city . . . .

CAEDMON'S HYMN

———— z ————

In the *Ecclesiastical History of the Nation of the Angles*, completed in 731, the Venerable Bede tells of an elderly lay brother called Caedmon at the abbey of Whitby presided over by St Hilda (d. 680). Though there must have been many before him, Caedmon is the first poet in English whose name is known to us, because he is the first Christian poet, and therefore worth Bede's preserving. Bede tells us that at a social evening the old man, seeing that the harp was getting near to him and that it would soon be his turn to perform, went out to see to the cattle, his task for the night. When he lay down to sleep, he dreamed that a man stood by him who called him by his name and told him to sing to him. Caedmon protested that he could not sing; but the man asked him to sing of the beginning of created things. Caedmon then sang a new set of verses in praise of the Creation. Bede gives a Latin version of *Caedmon's Hymn* (as it is called), several Old English versions of which are found among the 160 complete Latin manuscripts of the *Ecclesiastical History*. The first text below is in Early Northumbrian in a MS of 749. The second is in a Late West Saxon MS of the eleventh century. My translation follows.

Caedmon's Hymn

1. Nu scylun hergan   hefaenricaes uard,
   metudæs maecti   end his modgidanc,
   uerc uuldurfadur,   sue he uundra gihuaes,
   eci dryctin,   or astelidæ.
   He aerist scop   aelda barnum
   heben til hrofe,   haleg scepen;
   tha middungeard   moncynnæs uard,

5

    eci dryctin,   æfter tiadæ,
    firum foldu,   frea allmectig.

2. Nu we sculan herian   heofonrices Weard,
    Metodes mihte   and his modgeþonc,
    weorc Wuldorfæder;   swa he wundra gehwæs,
    ece Dryhten,   ord onstealde.
    He ærest gesceop   eorðan bearnum
    heofon to hrofe,   halig Scyppend:
    ða middongeard   moncynnes Weard,
    ece Dryhten,   æfter teode
    firum foldan,   Frea ælmihtig.

Praise now to the keeper of the kingdom of heaven,
the power of the Creator, the profound mind
of the glorious Father, who fashioned the beginning
of every wonder, the eternal Lord.
For the children of men he made first
heaven as a roof, the holy Creator.
Then the Lord of mankind, the everlasting Shepherd,
ordained in the midst as a dwelling place,
Almighty Lord, the earth for men.

BEDE'S DEATH SONG

———— z ————

AFTER Bede had died in 735, his disciple Cuthbert wrote in a letter that the dying man had sung the verse of St Paul the apostle telling of the fearfulness of falling into the hands of the living God (Hebrews 10. 31). Cuthbert adds that Bede had sung 'in our language also, as he was learned in our songs, speaking of the terrible departure of spirits from the body'. Cuthbert then gives the text in its original Northumbrian.

Bede's Death Song

Fore thaem neidfaerae   naenig uuirthit
thoncsnotturra,   than him tharf sie
to ymbhycggannae aer   his hiniongae
hwaet his gastae   godaes aeththae yflaes
aefter deothdaege   doemid uueorthae.

A literal prose version of this might be:

Before that sudden journey no one is wiser in thought than he needs to be, in considering, before his departure, what will be adjudged to his soul, of good or evil, after his death-day.

HEROIC POEMS: *DEOR* AND *WIDSITH*

———————— z ————————

DEOR

THE lament of the exiled poet, Deor, is unique among Anglo-Saxon poems in having a strophic form and a regular refrain. The recurrent *thæs ofereode, thisses swa mæg* is followed by a gap in the manuscript each time it is used, unlike the *ungelic is us* of *Wulf and Eadwacer*. *Deor* is also the only heroic poem with lyric form: each stanza is an epitome of a famous story, knotted and bitten off with *thæs ofereode, thisses swa mæg*. Usually, as Ker remarked, the movement of Anglo-Saxon heroic poetry is that of continuous narrative with a very deliberate forward sweep, 'the sense variously drawn out from one verse into another'. In *Deor*, as in the earliest poems (*Widsith*, the *Rune Poem*, and the *Charms*), the lines are end-stopped, not run on. The refrain is used with an effectiveness which must have been born of practice; and it may be that the lyric form was once as common in England as it was later in Scandinavia. The refrain is as 'untranslatable' as anything in Old English poetry.

Elliot van Kirk Dobbie gives a neat résumé of the mythic content of *Deor* in his introduction to *The Anglo-Saxon Poetic Records*, vol. III: 'The poem is cast in a monologue spoken by the minstrel Deor, formerly the *scop* of the Heodenings, who has been supplanted by one Heorrenda. As a salve to his own sorrows, Deor enumerates a series of misfortunes famous in Old Germanic heroic tradition: (1) the capture and mutilation of Wayland, corresponding to the story told in the *Völundarkviða* in the Poetic Edda, (2) the rape of Beadohild (by Wayland), who is the Böthvildr of the same poem, (3) a completely obscure reference to one Maethhild and (her lover?) Geat, (4) the exile of Theodoric the Ostrogoth, and (5) the tyranny of Ermanarich.' Each story is an example of misfortune outlived.

The penultimate stanza of *Deor* is longer than the others, is not followed by the usual refrain, and has a Christian tone which may seem out of place; but we have an insufficiently precise idea of what may have seemed consistent or inconsistent to an Anglo-Saxon audience to call this an interpolation. *Deor* is early, perhaps from the beginning of the eighth century; the language is, as usual, that of Alfred's Wessex, though there are some forms which may be Anglian.

WIDSITH

The 142 verses of *Widsith* are acknowledged to be the oldest in the English language, and form the earliest production in verse of any Germanic people. 'Read in a sympathetic mood, by anyone who has taken the trouble to acquaint himself with such of the old stories as time has left to us, *Widsith* demonstrates the dignity of the Old English narrative poetry, and of the common Germanic narrative poetry of which the Old English was but a section.' The truth of R. W. Chambers' estimate will not be doubted by anyone who has read this mysterious poem in his edition.[1] In his 260 pages he remedies our ignorance in a most able and even entertaining fashion. But without such an introduction, the poem has to be studied rather than read; I have tried to give the essentials in the notes to the poem.

Chambers sets forth some of the difficulties admirably: 'In *Widsith* we have a catalogue of some seventy tribes and of sixty-nine heroes, many of whom can be proved to have existed in the third, fourth, and fifth centuries of our era, and the latest of whom belong to the sixth century. Yet, although

---

[1] etc., refer the reader to the notes at the end of the book.

every chief whom we can date lived prior, not only to the conversion of the English to Christianity, but even to the completion of their settlement in Britain, this thoroughly heathen poem has come down to us in a transcript which some English monk made about the year 1000.'[2] Chambers' conclusions are that *Widsith* was probably composed in seventh-century Mercia, and continued in the reign of the Offa who built the Dyke along the Welsh Marches; but the poem deals exclusively with the period *previous* to the Anglian invasion of Britain, that is, with the heroic age: Widsith, 'the wide-traveller', accompanies Ealhhild, a Lombard princess, on her journey 'eastward from Angel' to the court of Eormanric the Goth. Ealhhild, the sister of Aelfwine, King of the Lombards, is made to marry Eormanric. But in fact the Gothic tyrant had been dead for two hundred years when Aelfwine (Alboin) was murdered in 573; and his court would have been somewhere between the Sea of Azov and the Danube. The geography of *Widsith* is legendary (apart from the placing of the tribes who lived on the coasts of the North Sea and the Baltic) and the chronology is elastic. But this does not mean that the poem has no historic value; apart from one long interpolation (printed here in square brackets) and one or two slight muddles perhaps introduced by a copyist, the information given in the poem is seriously intended and is an authentic reflection of the Anglian memories of their continental home and of the great, exemplary stories with which their minds were filled; there is only one fabulous name in the poem.[3] Widsith tells of the countries he went through and of the heroes he met. For the most part, these names are given in lists, but there are some – the most famous – whose stories are more fully told: Offa the Angle; the Danes, Hrothwulf and Hrothgar; Alboin the Lombard; Eormanric; and Eormanric's retinue, into which the most famous characters of Gothic history have been attracted – Eastgota, Theodoric, Widia and Hama.

On to this simple structure two considerable additions have been soldered – the first a list of the rulers of the Germanic tribes, the other a gratuitous supplement of biblical and other knowledge. This last interpolation, referred to above, was presumably made by a monk scribe very much later.

The catalogue of Germanic kings, beginning with the name of Attila, is of considerable antiquity, and probably antedates the composition of *Widsith* itself by several decades. Although it has no particular relevance at the beginning of Widsith's recital, and there are some inconsistencies[4] between it and situations described in the rest of the poem, this mnemonic catalogue of the folk-founders adds completeness to what was always intended as an evocation of the heroic world rather than an account of an actual journey. In the course of their wanderings until their ultimate settlement in the different parts of Europe, the members of the Germanic family of nations did not forget their kinship nor their common origins. An Anglian 'roll-call of dead lords' was not confined to Anglian heroes. The successes of the Goths against the Roman Empire were the glories of the German peoples; even the Huns played a part in their legends, though they were not a Germanic tribe.

At the risk of stating the obvious, one must repeat that the man or men who composed this poem, recently arrived from what used to be called Schleswig-Holstein, did not consider himself or themselves 'English'; and would certainly not have thought of 'the Continent' as 'foreign'. *Widsith* is like a list of the *dramatis personae* of all the Germanic heroic poems; to its audience every name was a name to conjure with. No *Who's Who* was necessary: these names were known in Iceland, in Wessex, on the Vistula and in the Viking settlement at the mouth of the Volga. To some of them we cannot today even supply a note; the poet's concluding advice to kings, that – if they wanted 'a name that should never die beneath the heavens' – they should give employment to poets, now sounds ironic. Yet we should not be studying this poem if there were not some truth in the claim.

A recapitulation of the 'plot' of *Widsith* may be of some help in deciphering it; the poem might be divided as follows:

Prologue: Widsith is introduced, and the story of his journey with Ealhhild to the Court of Eormanric, her future husband, is summarized.

The Catalogue of Germanic Kings: The Traveller announces his qualifications and gets down to the business of naming tribes and their founders. At the top of the German catalogue we find an unknown Hwala and Alexander the Great, who may have been added later. The mnemonic list begins with Attila and ends with Offa. It is noticeable that, apart from Huns, Goths, Greeks, and Burgundians, all the tribes mentioned come from the coasts of the Baltic and the North Seas. The stories of Offa the Angle and of Hrothgar and Hrothwulf, the kings of the neighbouring Danes, are given more fully.

The Second Catalogue: Widsith repeats his credentials and lists the tribes he has visited, again beginning with Huns and Goths, and again showing a good knowledge only of the north-west corner of Europe. Guthere the Burgundian and Aelfwine (Alboin the Lombard) are singled out for special praise.

The Interpolation (lines 75–87): Chambers suggests that a clerk copied *Widsith* mainly for its historical and geographical interest, and thought that it would not be complete without the mention of people who had since come within the horizon of common knowledge.

Ealhhild and Eormanric: A resumption of the story begun in the Prologue. Eormanric gives the minstrel a ring of extraordinary value, which Widsith presents to his lord, Eadgils, upon his return to his own country. Ealhhild also gives Widsith a ring before his departure, and the singer spreads the fame of her noble generosity.

The Followers of Eormanric: This is a catalogue of the most famous names in Gothic history and legend, concluding with references to the enmity of the Goths and the Huns, and to Widia and Hama, whose names survived into late medieval Germany poetry, and into Wagner. A brief résumé of the provenance of these names will be found in the Notes.

Epilogue: The end of the speech is followed by a fine passage on the wierd of the *scop* and his usefulness to society.

Deor

Wayland knew the wanderer's fate:
that single-willed earl suffered agonies,
sorrow and longing the sole companions
of his ice-cold exile. Anxieties bit
when Nithhad put a knife to his hamstrings,
laid clever bonds on the better man.

That went by; this may too.

Beadohild mourned her murdered brothers:
but her own plight pained her more
– her womb grew great with child.
When she knew that, she could never hold
steady before her wit what was to happen.

That went by; this may too.

All have heard of Hild's ravishing:
the Geat's lust was ungovernable,
their bitter love banished sleep.

That went by; this may too.

Thirty winters Theodric ruled
the Maering city: and many knew it.

That went by; this may too.

We all know that Eormanric
had a wolf's wit. Wide Gothland
lay in the grasp of that grim king,
and through it many sat, by sorrows environed,
foreseeing only sorrow; sighed for the downfall
and thorough overthrow of the thrall-maker.

That went by; this may too.

When each gladness has gone, gathering sorrow
may cloud the brain; and in his breast a man
can not then see how his sorrows shall end.

But he may think how throughout this world
it is the way of God, who is wise, to deal
to the most part of men much favour
and a flourishing fame; to a few the sorrow-share.

Of myself in this regard I shall say this only:
that in the hall of the Heodenings I held long the makarship,
lived dear to my prince, Deor my name;
many winters I held this happy place
and my lord was kind. Then came Heorrenda,
whose lays were skilful; the lord of fighting-men
settled on him the estate bestowed once on me.

That went by; this may too.

Widsith

This is the testimony of Widsith,
                    traveller through
kindreds and countries;
                    in courts he stood often,
knelt for the lovely stone,
                    no living man more often.
Unlocks his word-hoard.
                    (He went from the Myrgings
where his children were princes
                    with the peace-weaver,
the fair Ealhhild.
                    That was his first journey.
They went east from Angel
                    to Eormanric's halls
– the ruthless troth-breaker.)

                    His telling began thus:
'Of the master-rulers the most part have been known to me
and I say that any leader, any lord whosoever,
must live right, and rule his lands the same
if he wishes to come to a king's chair.
Of them all Hwala was for a while the best;
but Alexandreas' empire, of all I have heard of,
stretched furthest, and his strength flourished
more than that of any on earth I have heard of.

Attila ruled the Huns, Eormanric the Goths,
Becca the Banings, the Burgundians Gifeca,
Kaiser the Creeks, Caelic the Finns,
Hagena the Holm-Riggs, Heoden the Gloms;
Witta ruled the Swaefe, Wada the Halsings,
Meaca the Myrgings, Mearchealf the Hundings.

Theodric ruled the Franks, Thyle the Rondings,
Breca the Brondings, Billing the Werns;
Oswine ruled the Eows, and the Eats Getwulf,
Finn Folcwalding the Frisian kin,

16

Sigehere swayed the Sea-Danes long,
Hnaef the Hocings, Helm the Wulfings,
Wald the Woings, Wod the Thurings,
Seaferth the Seggs, the Swedes Ongentheow,
Shafthere the Ymbers, Sheafa the Longbeards,
Hun the Hetwars, Holen the Wrosns,
Ringweald was the name of the Raiders' chief.

Offa ruled Angel, Alewih the Danes;
he was of all these men the most courageous,
yet he did not outdo Offa in valour:
before all men Offa stands,
having in boyhood won the broadest of kingdoms;
no youngster did work worthier of an earl.
With single sword he struck the boundary
against the Myrgings where it marches now,
fixed it at Fifeldor. Thenceforward it has stood
between Angles and Swaefe where Offa set it.

Hrothgar and Hrothwulf held their bond
– father's brother and brother's son –
long after their victory over the viking clan
when they made Ingeld's edge bow,
hewed down at Heorot the Heathobard troop.

So fared I on through foreign lands
over the ground's breadth. Both good and evil
I came to know there; of no kinship,
from family far, I followed many.
So I may sing, and stories tell;
I call in hall rehearse before the gathering
how men of kingly birth were kinglike towards me.

I was among the Huns and among the Hreth-Goths
among Swedes, among Geats and among South Danes,
among Verns I was, among Vikings, and among Vendels,
among Gepids I was, among Wends, and among Gefflegs,
among Angles I was, among Swaefe, and among Aenenes,
among Saxons I was, among Seggs, and among Swordmen,

among Whalemen I was, among Deans, and among War-
                                                    Reams
with the men of Throndheim I was, and with Thuringians,
and among the Burgundians. I got there a ring,
Guthere gave me the gleaming token,
a bright stone for a song. He was not slow to give.
With Franks I was, with Frisians, and among Frumtings,
with Rugians I was, with Gloms, and among Rome-Welsh.

I was with Aelfwine in Italy too.
In my wanderings I've not met with a man whose hand
faster framed a fame-winning deed,
or who gave rings with gladder face
than Edwin's bairn did the bright arm-bands.

[Among Saracens I was, and among Serings I was,
among Finns, among Creeks, and with Kaiser I was,
who was the wielder of wine-filled cities,
and rent and riches, and the Roman domain.
I was with Picts and with Scots and with Sliding-Finns,
with Leons and with Bretons and with Langobards,
with heathens and with heroes and with Hundings,
with the Israelites I was, and with the Exsyringians,
with Ebrews, with Indians, and with the Egyptians,
among Medes I was, and with Persians, with Myrgings,
and with the Mofdings *against* the Myrgings,
and among Amothings. With East Thuringians I was,
with Eols and with Ests and among Idumings.]

And I was with Eormanric all the days
that the Goth King was kind towards me:
lord over cities and they who lived in them.
Six hundred shillings' worth of sheer gold
were wound into the ring he reached to my hand.
(I owed it to Eadgils, overlord of the Myrgings,
my king and keeper, and at my coming home
I gave it him against a grant of land
formerly bestowed on me, the estate of my father.)

Ealhhild also, before all the company
gave me another, Edwin's daughter;
and when the name was asked of the noblest girl,
gold-hung queen, gift-dealer,
beneath the sky's shifting – the most shining lady –
I sang Ealhhild; in every land
I spoke her name, spread her fame.
When we struck up the lay before our lord in war,
Shilling and I, with sheer-rising voices,
the song swelling to the sweet-touched harp,
many men there of unmelting hearts,
who well knew, worded their thought,
said this was the best song sung in their hearing.

I travelled through every quarter of the kingdoms of the
                                        Goths,
kept company only with clear-headed men.
Such might always be found among the fellows of Eormanric.
Hethca I sought out, Beadeca, and the Herelings:
I found Emerca and Fridla, and Eastgota
the father of Unwen, no fool but a good man.
I came to Secca & Becca, was with Seafola & Theodric,
Heathoric & Sifeca, Hlitha & Ongentheow.
I sought Eadwine, Elsa, Aegelmund, Hungar,
and the brave band of the Broad-Myrgings.
Wulfhere I sought, and Wormhere; war did not often slacken
                                          there
when the Gothic host with hard swords
had to defend in the forests of the Vistula
their ancient hearthland against Attila's people.

I sought out Raedhere, Rondhere, Rumstan & Gislhere.
Withergield & Freotheric, and Widia and Hama,
– the worst of comrades they were not either,
though I have not named them first.
Whining and whistling, wooden shafts
streamed from their company, stooped on the enemy.

It was Widia and Hama who wielded the people,
two strangers distributed the gold.

In faring the roads I have found this true,
that among earth-dwellers the dearest men
are those whom God lends his lordship over others.'

The makar's wierd is to be a wanderer:
the poets of mankind go through the many countries,
speak their needs, say their thanks.
Always they meet with someone, in the south lands or the
                                                            north,

who understands their art, an open-handed man
who would not have his fame fail among the guard
nor rest from an earl's deeds before the end cuts off
light and life together.
                        Lasting honour shall be his,
a name that shall never die beneath the heavens.

HEROIC POEMS: *BEOWULF* AND *THE FIGHT AT FINNSBURG*

———— *z* ————

BEOWULF is the story of a dragon-slayer. The hero, a Geat, hears that a man-eating monster called Grendel has been terrorizing Heorot, the hall of Hrothgar, King of the Danes. He sails to Denmark, kills Grendel, and has then to kill Grendel's mother, who lives at the bottom of a pool on the moors. Thanked and rewarded by Hrothgar, Beowulf sails home and fights for his own king, Hygelac, against the Swedes. Later he himself becomes king of the Geats, and after a reign of fifty years, saves his people by killing a fire-breathing dragon. Mortally wounded in the fight, he dies with his eyes on the dragon's hoard. The poem ends with the Geats lamenting around his barrow.

This bald synopsis should be enough for the reader unacquainted with *Beowulf* to place the five extracts here translated. To choose five meagre passages may seem an arbitrary way of representing *Beowulf*; but, while one can not honestly exclude altogether the poem which shows Anglo-Saxon versification at its fullest and richest, to have translated more would not have been to my purpose in this book. I hope the passages will stand, so far as is possible, on their own. They are: the funeral of Scyld; Beowulf's voyage; the Danes' visit to the mere; the 'Lay of the Last Survivor', and Beowulf's funeral.

The Funeral of Scyld Shefing. The scribe of *Beowulf* divides his manuscripts into fitts, or sections. Before Fitt I, which begins at line 53, there is a prologue which tells of the coming of Scyld to Denmark: he is found a helpless child and lives to unite the Danes under the Scylding house, to whom all the surrounding tribes have to pay tribute. This father of his people (and great-grandfather of Hrothgar) eventually dies, full of years; at which point my extract begins.

21

We are not told exactly how Scyld arrived in Denmark, but the story is similar to others in which a child with his head pillowed on a sheaf of corn is borne ashore in a ship.[1] At the end of his life the foundling founder of the Danes is, like Arthur, returned to the unknown: he is given a ship-burial. Ship-burial was common from the Bronze Age onwards, and there is plenty of archaeological evidence for it in Scandinavia. But the most striking confirmation of the historicity of this description was the finding, in 1939, of a considerable number of objects of great richness and beauty in the remains of a ship buried in a barrow in Suffolk. The coins in the purse in the Sutton Hoo treasure indicate that it dates from about 650; *Beowulf* is thought to have been written a century or so later. It is remarkable that the ship at Sutton Hoo contained golden armour, shield, and standard, all specifically mentioned in the description of Scyld's burial; they are now to be seen, together with the rest of this royal treasure, in the British Museum. It seems likely that the Sutton Hoo ship was meant as a cenotaph − a pagan memorial, perhaps to the Christian Anna, King of the East Angles.[2]

Scyld, if he was a historical character − and there is no reason to suppose that the Scylding royal house did not have a founder − would have lived in the fourth century, centuries before Christianity, and he might certainly have had a burial just like that described in the poem. He is introduced here as the archetypal folk-founder, the great-grandfather of Hrothgar, who is to play the chief part in the first half of *Beowulf*. Perhaps it is no accident that the poem both opens and closes with a funeral.[3]

Beowulf's Voyage to Denmark. Geatland was in southern Sweden − the modern Götarike. Heorot was probably near modern Lejre on the north coast of Zealand, not far from Roskilde.[4]

The sea-voyage was a natural choice for an extract from *Beowulf*; but I have also translated the coastguard's speech to show the formality and pleasant courtesy of manners in the

poem, much like that at the court of Alcinous in the *Odyssey*.[5]
In his answer to the coastguard, Beowulf explains that they
are a party of Geats, that he is Edgethew's son, that their
errand is friendly. The coastguard welcomes them and escorts
them to Heorot, leaving a guard over the ship; arrived at the
hall, he bids them farewell. The Geats are then greeted by
Hrothgar's herald; the same exchanges of name and office are
made, and the herald announces their arrival to Hrothgar.
Hrothgar reminisces about his old friend Edgethew, and then
sends out the herald to fetch in the Geats; he and Beowulf
exchange long speeches. So the poet displays his knowledge of
court usage and his skill at constructing a developing series of
encounters. The whole of oral poetry is built out of such
units.

The Mere. The Danes ride to inspect the mere, to make sure
that Grendel is well and truly dead. As they return the *scop*
composes, on horseback, a lay of Beowulf (see Introduction,
p. xii).

'*The Lay of the Last Survivor*.' Beowulf has been king of the
Geat people for a long time. We hear of a dragon who lives
in a barrow up on the heath: a fugitive stumbles into the
barrow and steals a piece of the treasure while the dragon is
asleep. The poet then begins on a description of the hoard,
and suddenly side-slips into giving us the imagined thoughts
of the last survivor of the race that amassed this treasure, as he
carries it piece by piece into the tumulus – hundreds of years
before. This grand passage shows many similarities with the
'elegies' – especially *The Ruin* and *The Wanderer*. It also shows
that the time-shift, with the hallucinatory effect that it brings,
was not a discovery of French novelists.

Beowulf's Funeral. After Beowulf has died in the fight with the
Dragon, his people, now bereft of his protection, give him a
funeral and place his ashes in a barrow, together with the
Dragon's gold. The poem closes with their epitaph.

THE FIGHT AT FINNSBURG

The only text of this fragment appears in George Hickes'
*Linguarum Veterum Septentrionalium Thesaurus Grammatico-
Criticus et Archaeologicus* (Oxoniae, 1705). Hickes found it
on a leaf bound up with a collection of homilies in Lambeth
Palace library; this leaf has unfortunately been lost.

The fragment is the story of a night attack made on a hall
and of the five days' defence made by Hnaef and his men. But
why the attack was made, or by whom, would not have been
known without the evidence of the Finn lay in *Beowulf*. The
night after the Danes return from the mere (my third extract),
King Hrothgar gives a banquet for the Geats and makes many
presents to Beowulf. The Danish *scop* sings a lay; the entertain-
ment (*heal-gamen*) takes the form of a tale from the Danish
past, the tale of Finn's treachery and of Hengest's successful re-
venge.

The story is a complicated one, more complicated than that
of *Beowulf* itself, although the *Beowulf* poet sums it up in less
than a hundred lines. His listeners must be assumed to have
known the tale already, for some of the allusions are cryptic
indeed. The outline given by Professor Wrenn in his edition
of *Beowulf* is the one now generally accepted. It runs as follows:
Hnaef, leader of the Danes, is staying in a hall at Finnsburg,
visiting his sister, Hildburg, who is married to Finn, the Frisian
chief. The fight described in the fragment takes place; Hnaef
is killed, and Hengest takes his place: but Finn cannot over-
come the Danish resistance and has to call a truce. Hengest's
terms for submission to Finn are that the Danes shall have
equal rights with Finn's own followers.

One winter, years later, Hunlafing lays a sword across the
knees of Hengest: it is a reminder of the vengeance due for
Hnaef. Accordingly, in the spring Hengest sends Oslaf and
Guthlaf (the Ordlaf and Guthlaf of the Fragment)[6] back to
Denmark; there they collect some men, sail back to Finnsburg,
and make a slaughter of King Finn and his Frisians. They take
Hildburg home to Denmark.

The motive for Finn's original attack is not given, but we can assume that there is a feud of long standing between Frisians and Danes. Such unappeasable feuds are common in Old English literature and the recorded history of Anglo-Saxon England; also typical of lay and saga is the effort to patch up peace by means of a marriage. The marriage of Ealhhild to Eormanric in *Widsith* is a case in point. But the blood-feud lingered on from generation to generation; Miss Whitelock cites some recorded cases.[7] Neither priest nor king could exorcize in Anglo-Saxon times (and even under the Normans, who were ancestrally Norsemen) the deeply-held feeling that to avenge one's own kinsman was an absolute duty and that to take *wergild* instead of blood was shameful. Tacitus tells us that 'a man is bound to take up the feuds as well as the friendships of father or kinsman. But feuds do not continue unreconciled. Even homicide can be atoned for by a fixed number of cattle or sheep.' This shows that the practice of *wergild* – the gold a man was worth to his kin – was very ancient. But Tacitus also tells us that among the Germans of his time 'to leave a battle alive after your chief has fallen . . . means lifelong infamy and shame.' There is no doubt that Hengest's action was approved of.[8]

The fragment begins in the middle of a speech by a man guarding the door of Hnaef's hall.

Beowulf

THE FUNERAL OF SCYLD SHEFING (lines 26–52)

At the hour shaped for him Scyld departed,
the many-strengthed moved into his Master's keeping.

They carried him out to the current sea,
his sworn arms-fellows, as he himself had asked
while he wielded by his words, Ward of the Scyldings,
beloved folk-founder; long had he ruled.

A boat with a ringed neck rode in the haven,
icy, out-eager, the aetheling's vessel,
and there they laid out their lord and master,
dealer of wound gold, in the waist of the ship,
in majesty by the mast.
                        A mound of treasures
from far countries was fetched aboard her,
and it is said that no boat was ever more bravely fitted out
with the weapons of a warrior, war accoutrement,
bills and byrnies; on his breast were set
treasures and trappings to travel with him
on his far faring into the flood's sway.

This hoard was not less great than the gifts he had
from those who sent him, on the sill of life,
over seas, alone, a small child.

High over head they hoisted and fixed
a gold *signum*; gave him to the flood,
let the seas take him, with sour hearts
and mourning moods. Men have not the knowledge
to say with any truth – however tall beneath the heavens,
however much listened to – who unloaded that boat.

BEOWULF'S VOYAGE TO DENMARK (lines 194–257)

Grendel was known of then in Geatland across the sea
to one of Hygelac's followers, the first of his thanes
and for main strength of all men first
that trod ground at the time being;
build and blood matched.

He bade a seaworthy
wave-cutter be fitted out for him; the warrior king
he would seek, he said, over swan's riding,
that lord of name, needing men.

The wiser sought to dissuade him from voyaging
hardly or not at all, though they held him dear;
whetted his quest-thirst, watched omens.

The prince had already picked his men
from the folk's flower, the fiercest among them
that might be found. With fourteen men
sought sound-wood: sea-wise Beowulf
led them right down to the land's edge.

Time running on, she rode the waves now
hard in by headland. Harnessed warriors
stepped on her stem; setting tide churned
sea with sand, soldiers carried
bright mail-coats to the mast's foot,
war-gear well wrought; willingly they shoved her out,
thorough-braced craft, on the craved voyage.

Away she went over a wavy ocean
boat like a bird, breaking seas,
wind-whetted, white-throated,
till curved prow had ploughed so far
– the sun standing right on the second day –
that they might see land loom on the skyline,
then the shimmer of cliffs, sheer moors behind,
reaching capes.

The crossing was at an end;

closed the wake. Weather-Geats
stood on strand, stepped briskly up;
a rope going ashore, ring-mail clashed,
battle-girdings. God they thanked
for the smooth going over the salt-trails.
The watchman saw them. From the wall where he stood,
posted by the Scyldings to patrol the cliffs,
he saw the polished lindens pass along the gangway
and the clean equipment. Curiosity
moved him to know who these men might be.

Hrothgar's thane, when his horse had picked
its way down to the shore, shook his spear
fiercely at arm's length, framed the challenge:
'Strangers, you have steered this steep craft
through the sea-ways, sought our coast.
I see you are warriors; you wear that dress now.
I must ask who you are. In all the years
I have lived as look-out at land's end here
– so that no foreigners with a fleet-army
might land in Denmark and do us harm –
shield-carriers have never come ashore
more openly. You had no assurance
of welcome here, word of leave
from Hrothgar and Hrothwulf!

                        I have not in my life
set eyes on a man with more might in his frame
than this helmed lord. That's no hall-fellow
worthied with weapons; or well counterfeited,
for he has a hero's look.

                  I must have your names now
and the names of your fathers; or further you shall not go
as undeclared spies into the Danish land.

Stay where you are, strangers, hear
what I have to say! Seas crossed,
it is best and simplest straightaway to acknowledge
where you are from, why you have come.'

THE MERE (lines 837–75)

There was, as I heard it, at hall next morning
a great gathering in gift-hall yard
to see the wonder. Along wide highroads
the clanchiefs came from close and far away
onto the killer's trail; and with truth it may be said
that there was not among them one man sorry
to see the spoor-blood of that blind rush
for the monster's mere, when his mood had sickened
with every step-stagger, strength broken,
dragging deathwards his dribbling life.

The tarn was troubled; a terrible wave-thrash
brimmed it, bubbling; black-mingled,
the warm wound-blood welled upwards.
Here the death-marked dived, here died with no gladness;
in the fen-moor lair he laid aside
his heathen soul. Hell welcomed it.

Then the older retainers turned back on the way
journeyed so joyfully; joined by the young men,
warriors on white horses wheeled away from the mere
in bold mood. Beowulf's feat
was much spoken of, and many said
that between the seas, south or north,
over earth's stretch no other man
beneath sky's shifting excelled Beowulf,
of all sword-wielders worthiest of empire.
In saying this they did not slight in the least
the gracious Hrothgar, for he was a good king.

Where as they went their way broadened
they would match their mounts, making them leap
along the best stretches, the strife-eager
on their fallow horses.

Or a fellow of the king's
whose head was a storehouse of the storied verse,
whose tongue gave gold to the language
of the treasured repertory, wrought a new lay
made in the measure.
                    The man struck up,
found the phrase, framed rightly
the deed of Beowulf, drove the tale,
rang word-changes. He chose to speak
first of Sigemund, sang the most part
of what he had heard of that hero's exploits. . . .

'THE LAY OF THE LAST SURVIVOR' (lines 2231–66)

There were heaps of hoard-things in this hall underground
which once in gone days gleamed and rang;
the treasure of a race rusts derelict.

In another age an unknown man,
brows bent, brought and hid here
the beloved hoard. The whole race
death-rapt, and of the ring of earls
one left alive; living on in that place
heavy with friend-loss, the hoard-guard
waited the same wierd. His wit acknowledged
that the treasures gathered and guarded over the years
were his for the briefest while.
                    Barrow stood ready
on flat ground where breakers beat at the headland,
new, near at hand, made narrow of access.
The keeper of rings carried into it
the earls' holdings, the hoard-worthy part
fraught with gold, few words spoke:
'Hold, ground, the gold of the earls!
Men could not. Cowards they were not
who took it from thee once, but war-death took them,
that stops life, struck them, spared not one

man of my people, passed on now.
They have had their hall-joys. I have not with me
a man able to unsheathe this. . . .
Who shall polish this plated vessel?
This cup was dear. The company is elsewhere.

This hardened helmet healed with gold
shall lose its shell. They sleep now
whose work was to burnish the battle-mask;
so the cuirass that in the crash took
bite of iron amid breaking shields:
it moulders with the man. This mailshirt travelled far,
hung from a shoulder shouldered warriors;
it shall not jingle again.
               There's no joy from harp-play,
gleewood's gladness, no good hawk
swings through hall now, no swift horse
tramps at threshold. The threat came:
falling has felled a flowering kingdom.'

BEOWULF'S FUNERAL (lines 3137–82)

The Geat race then reared up for him
a funeral pyre. It was not a petty mound,
but shining mail-coats and shields of war
and helmets hung upon it, as he had desired.
Then the heroes, lamenting, laid out in the middle
their great chief, their cherished lord.
On top of the mound the men then kindled
the biggest of funeral-fires. Black wood-smoke
arose from the blaze, and the roaring of flames
mingled with weeping. The winds lay still
as the heat at the fire's heart consumed
the house of bone. And in heavy mood
they uttered their sorrow at the slaughter of their lord.

A woman of the Geats in grief sang out

the lament for his death. Loudly she sang,
her hair bound up, the burden of her fear
that evil days were destined her
– troops cut down, terror of armies,
bondage, humiliation. Heaven swallowed the smoke.

Then the Storm–Geat nation constructed for him
a stronghold on the headland, so high and broad
that seafarers might see it from afar.
The beacon to that battle-reckless man
they made in ten days. What remained from the fire
they cast a wall around, of workmanship
as fine as their wisest men could frame for it.
They placed in the tomb both the torques and the jewels,
all the magnificence that the men had earlier
taken from the hoard in hostile mood.
They left the earls' wealth in the earth's keeping,
the gold in the dirt. It dwells there yet,
of no more use to men than in ages before.

Then the warriors rode around the barrow,
twelve of them in all, athelings' sons.
They recited a dirge to declare their grief,
spoke of the man, mourned their King.
They praised his manhood and the prowess of his hands,
they raised his name; it is right a man
should be lavish in honouring his lord and friend,
should love him in his heart when the leading-forth
from the house of flesh befalls him at last.

This was the manner of the mourning of the men of the
                                                    Geats,
sharers in the feast, at the fall of their lord:
they said that he was of all the world's kings
the gentlest of men, and the most gracious,
the kindest to his people, the keenest for fame.

The Fight at Finnsburg

'. . . the horns of the house, hall-gables burning?'

Battle-young Hnaef broke silence:
'It is not the eaves aflame, nor in the east yet
does day break; no dragon flies this way.
It is the soft clashing of claymores you hear
that they carry to the house.

               Soon shall be the cough of birds,
hoar wolf's howl, hard wood-talk,
shield's answer to shaft.

             Now shines the moon,
welkin-wanderer. The woes at hand
shall bring to the full this folk's hatred for us.

'Awake! on your feet! Who fights for me?
Hold your lindens right, hitch up your courage,
think bravely, be with me at the doors!'

The gold-clad thanes rose, girt on their swords.
Two doubtless soldiers stepped to the door,
Sigeferth and Eaha, with their swords out,
and Ordlaf and Guthlaf to the other door went,
Hengest himself hastening in their steps.

Hearing these adversaries advance on the door
Guthere held on to Garulf so he should not
front the rush to force the threshold
and risk his life, whose loss could not be remedied;
but clear above their whispers he called out his demand,
– brave heart – Who held the door?

'My name is Sigeferth, of the Secgan, chief,
known through the seas. I have seen a few battles
and known troubles. What you intend for me
your own flesh shall be the first to taste.'

Then swung strokes sounded along the wall;
wielded by the brave, the bone-shielding

boss-boards split. Burg-floor spoke,
and Garulf fell at last in the fighting at the door,
Garulf, the first man in the Frisian islands,
son to Guthlaf, and good men lay around,
a pale crowd of corpses. The crows dangled
black and brown. Blades clashing
flashed fire – as though all Finnsburg were ablaze.

Never have sixty swordmen in a set fight
borne themselves more bravely; or better I have not heard of.
Never was the bright mead better earned
than that which Hnaef gave his guard of youth.

They fought and none fell. On the fifth day
the band was still whole and still held the doors.
Then a wounded warrior went to the side,
said his ring-coat was riven to pieces,
stout hauberk though it was, and that his helm had gone
                                        through.
The folk's shepherd and shielder asked him
how the braves bore their wounds
and which of the young men. . . .

HEROIC POEMS: *WALDERE*

———————— z ————————

THE story of Walter of Aquitaine is a good one, and must have been well known; there are extant versions of it in Anglo-Saxon, German, Latin and Polish. The Anglo-Saxon fragments, in the writing of the year 1000, were found in the Royal Library at Copenhagen in 1860; it is supposed that these vellum pages had been deposited there by Thorkelin, an Icelandic scholar who had come to England fifty years earlier to make a transcript of *Beowulf*. The only other early version of the story is *Waltharius*, a Latin verse epic written by Ekkehard I, a monk of St Gall, in about the year 930. These and the later versions are thought to derive eventually from a Bavarian lay of the early seventh century. One of the many difficulties of *Waldere* is to determine how much of the story as we have it in *Waltharius* is original, so that we may construct a skeleton for the *membra disiecta* of *Waldere*.

Norman has a useful synopsis of *Waltharius* in his edition of *Waldere*; I reproduce it here.

Attila, king of the Huns, made war on the western nations. Franks, Burgundians and Aquitanians submitted to the Hunnish yoke and offered hostages. Gibicho, king of the Franks, sent Hagano;[1] Heriricus, king of the Burgundians, sent his only daughter Hiltgunt; Alphere, king of Aquitania, sent his only son Waltharius who was betrothed to Hiltgunt. Attila returned home. The strangers were well treated yet they longed for freedom. When Gibicho died and his son Guntharius refused to pay the tribute, Hagano fled. Attila feared that Waltharius, who had become a famous champion and the leader of his army, might also flee. Queen Ospirin suggested a Hunnish marriage; Waltharius saw that he must escape. After a successful campaign he invited Attila, Ospirin, and the Hunnish nobles to a banquet. Hiltgunt collected two chests full of treasure, Waltharius armed himself and they fled [on one horse] whilst the

Huns were sleeping off their intoxication. Attila offered rich rewards, but none dared pursue them. They lived on fish and birds, travelled by night and reached the Rhine after forty days. There they made a present of some strange fish to the ferryman. These reached the table of Guntharius and so it became known that Waltharius had returned. The king, seeing a chance for plunder, set out with eleven armed knights. Hagano, whose warnings were not heeded, accompanied him unwillingly. Meanwhile, Waltharius had reached the Vosges and had camped for the night. Hiltgunt woke him as the strangers approached. Hagano once more gave warning and then drew aside. Waltharius made offerings of peace – a hundred rings, two hundred rings – but they were refused, and so they fought. Protected by the defile in which he had camped, he could only be attacked from the front. He killed eight knights in single combat. Then three knights set upon him, throwing a trident with a rope tied to it. It lodged in his shield and the three, with Guntharius, tried to pull him from his stronghold. Waltharius bided his time, then, letting go his shield, fell upon the knights and slew them. Guntharius barely escaped.

In the battle Hagano's nephew had been slain and Hagano agreed at last to fight his old companion. He and Guntharius lay in wait for him next morning and attacked him in the open. In the fight the king lost a leg. To save the death-blow Hagano threw his body between the combatants. Waltharius' sword was broken and his right hand cut off. Then, fighting with a short sword in his left, he took out one of Hagano's eyes and six of his teeth. That was the end of the contest. Hiltgunt attended to the wounds. Hagano and the king went back to Worms and Hiltgunt and Waltharius to their home. After his marriage Waltharius reigned for thirty years.

The first Anglo-Saxon fragment is a robust speech of encouragement addressed to Waldere, obviously spoken by Hildeguth. She speaks of 'many foes' and of Waldere's recklessness in leaving his position; we may fairly take this as referring to an episode similar to that of the trident in *Waltharius*. She then says that Guthere will be punished for his refusal to accept the rings; so we may assume that the fight between Waldere and Guthere and Hagen has not yet taken place, and that these words are spoken in the interval in the fighting, perhaps during the night, one of the lovers resting while the other keeps watch. The only point to be commented on here is the mention of Waldere's sword, Mimming, a blade of

Wayland's manufacture. Hildeguth tells Waldere he need have no anxiety, Mimming will prove better than Guthere's sword. (Famous swords always have names in Germanic heroic poetry, and we hear of Mimming in medieval German lays: Theodric von Bern gives it to Widia, the son of Wayland, as a reward for helping him escape from the Giants. How does Waldere come to have Mimming? In the second fragment the poet says that he knows that Theodric *meant* to present Mimming to Widia, but omits to explain why he did not do so.[2])

Fragment II consists of two speeches, one in praise of a sword, the other a challenge by Waldere to Guthere: is the Burgundian king afraid, now that Hagen has refused to help him, to relieve Waldere's battle-wearied shoulders of the weight of the armour left him by Aelfhere? The last sentence of this second speech is a stiff genuflection to the Lord, 'who shall give victory'; it has a hollow ring and I have presumed to omit it.

The first speech of Fragment II begins in mid-sentence, and different scholars have attributed it to Waldere, to Guthere and to Hagen. I have accepted Norman's arguments[3] in favour of giving the speech to Waldere, though they are not conclusive; they involve the assumption that in the middle of this fragment Waldere pauses for breath before delivering his taunt to Guthere. The words immediately previous to the first speech must have been a boast that the speaker had the best sword in the world – 'except one only, which he also has'. This fits in with the fact that the hero of *Waltharius* has two swords.

The unfamiliarity of the names, and the doubts about who is speaking in Fragment II, must not detract from the quality of *Waldere*. The dramatic potentialities of the lovers' flight, the fight in the pass, and the conflict in Hagen's breast between his friendship for Waldere and his allegiance to Guthere (one typical of Old English poetry, and even more typical in that it is resolved by a third claim, that of vengeance for a nephew) – all these make it regrettable that there is not enough of *Waldere* for us to make a fair comparison with *Beowulf*.[4]

Waldere

I

   . . . Hildeguth, heartening him:
'Never shall work of Wayland fail
a master of Mimming, a man who knows
the handling of that blade. Bleeding from its wounds,
lords and aethelings are laid on the field.

Right hand of Attila, let not your royal strength
droop now, nor your daring – now that the day has come
when, son of Aelfhere, you shall surely either
give over living or a long doom
have among after-men, one or other.

Never shall my tongue tell to your shame
that I saw my friend at the sword play
with a fainting valour falter before the attack
of any man whatever, or make for the baulk
to save his neck – though new foes came
and reaching blades rang on his breast.

No, you carried the fight so far into the open
that I dreaded your death. You drove on too boldly,
crowding the strike – with each step further
out of your ground. God is with you:
you may enrich your name with less reckless strokes.

And mourn not for the sword; Mimming was tempered
and given to this end, that Guthere's wrong
in provoking this fight should be proved by the outcome,
and on it his vaunts should by you be invalidated.
He would not take sword, nor silver chests,
nor the mass of arm-bands. Bare-armed then
shall he turn from this field, trail homeward
to the land he left; unless he rest here . . .'

II

'. . . better
except one only, which I also have
still fast in its sheath, as sharp as ever.
I know that Theodric once thought to send it
to Widia himself, and along with the blade
a wealth of treasure and a troop in escort
all clad in gold – as a gift, because
in a narrow place once Nithhad's grandson
– the lord Widia, Wayland's son –
had saved Theodric, and through him
the Goth slipped the guard of the Giants.'

Again Waldere unwavering spoke,
held in hand his help in battle,
his cleaver keenly ground, called out these words:
'*Hwaet!* King of Burgundians, did you count on
the hand of Hagen? Was it he who was to finish
Waldere's fighting days?
                        I am weary of fighting:
you may come and collect my casings, if you dare.
It is a good, bossed, gold-studded coat
that lies across my shoulders, left me by Aelfhere,
in every way worth an aetheling's wearing
if he has enemies against whom
he must guard his life's hoard. It has not let me down
when untrue kinsmen have betrayed me
and turned swords on me, as yourselves have done . . .'

ELEGIES: *THE WANDERER AND THE SEAFARER*

———— *z* ————

EXILE is a theme of the more personal poetry of Anglo-Saxon England, as it is of ancient Chinese poetry. An exile (*wraecca*, also meaning 'wretch, stranger, wanderer, pilgrim, unhappy man') is the protagonist of all the Old English elegies. Why is this so?

One must consider the conditions of the old heroic model of society: it was organized in small units; and the unit, the *cynn*, was organized around its lord. These communities were truly united – to a degree we would find claustrophobic. The men of the *cynn*, all more or less related to one another, as they gathered round their lord in the smoky hall at supper, shared the same food and drink, just as, during the day, they shared much the same tasks, whatever their rank. In Anglo-Saxon communities, though there was of course distinction of classes, there was no snobbery. The dangers which men had originally banded together to overcome – animals, elements, enemies, hunger, disease – were never far enough away for the essential identity of interest to disintegrate. The *cynn* made man's life less cheap than beast's: a man without a lord was orphaned, outcast. *Hlaford*, the Anglo-Saxon word for 'lord', is derived from *hlaf-weard*, the guardian of the loaf, the provider of bread, the incarnation of the life-principle of an agricultural society. The meal in the mead-hall, at which he presided, was a celebration of the success of human society: all Old English poetry refers to 'the joys of the mead-hall'. Tacitus observed that 'no nation abandons itself more completely to banqueting than the German' and that 'drinking-bouts lasting a day and a night are considered in no way disgraceful'. It would not be far from the truth to say that the passing round of the horn filled with beer was the most important heroic ritual.

But a man got more than food and a feeling of solidarity from his lord and his king; as Miss Whitelock says, 'he got protection. No one would be eager to molest a man who had a powerful lord ready to demand compensation or to take vengeance. The lord took responsibility for the man's acts; he had to produce him to answer a charge in court, or pay the damages himself, and it would be to his interest to defend his man from a wrongful accusation. He was held responsible even for deeds committed before the man entered his service, and would therefore be unwise too readily to accept an unknown man. This may explain why in the poem *The Wanderer* the man bereft of his lord finds it so difficult to find a new protector. The lord's responsibility for his followers is the aspect of this relationship which stands out most prominently in the laws.'[1]

No one story gives a better impression of the temper of those times or forms a more appropriate introduction to these elegiac poems than that which Bede tells of King Edwin of Northumbria and of his conversion by Paulinus. In the year 625 Paulinus brought the Gospel across the Humber, and Edwin, 'being a man of unusual wisdom', summoned a Council:

And one of the King's chief men presently said: 'Thus seems it to me, thou King, the present life of man on earth against that time which is unknown to us: it is as if thou wert sitting at a feast with thy chief men and thy thanes in the winter-time; the fire burns and the hall is warmed, and outside it rains and snows and storms. Comes a sparrow and swiftly flies through the house; it comes through one door and goes out another. Lo, in the time in which he is within he is not touched by the winter storm, but that time is the flash of an eye and the least of times, and he soon passes from winter to winter again. So is the life of man revealed for a brief space, but what went before and what follows after we know not.'

So spoke Coifi, chief of the pagan priests, and upon hearing that the new Word would tell of what went before and what follows after, he mounted upon horseback and rode, spear in hand, to the demolishing of the idol-altars. So Margaret Williams tells the story in her *Word-Hoard*, using not the Latin of the *Ecclesiastical History* but the Old English version associated with Alfred the Great.[2]

This picture of the hall, and of the impact of Christianity upon a people who could not be other than aware that life is at best a temporary affair, goes a long way to explain the recurrent and frequently unreconciled contrast which the elegies always point between the *wraecca* and the *cynn*, the firelit, gold-adorned, beer-warm hall and the exterior darkness of sea and moor. Their pessimism about this life is as unmitigated and inescapable as Hardy's; and, two hundred years after Paulinus, they are not quite sure of 'what follows after'.

Although *The Wanderer* and *The Seafarer* are separated by two leaves in The Exeter Book, they deal with similar themes and present similar difficulties. The speaker in both is a *wraecca* – 'allone, withouten any compaignye'. The difficulty in both is, first, one of punctuation: the poems are written out as prose, and such pointing as there is is sporadic and inconsistent. So there is no knowing where speeches begin or end. Partly as a consequence of this, there is a big editorial problem: judged by the usual criteria of today, which are those of a rationalist literary tradition, *The Wanderer* and *The Seafarer* lack thematic coherence. They do not resolve 'inconsistencies'.

It is natural to suppose that when oral poetry was first committed to script it was still intended to be spoken aloud, though the poet himself might not be present. The manuscript was a text for oral performance; hence poetry conserved its oral style, more or less.

Now, an oral style needs traditional material, otherwise it loses its shape. The heroic poems are held together by their given story. Even the elegies, *The Wanderer* and *The Seafarer* apart, deal with traditional themes: *The Ruin*, 'The Lay of the

Last Survivor', *The Husband's Message*, and the others, all are organized by the nature of their material – either a ready-made dramatic situation or a descriptive set-piece. But *The Wanderer* and *The Seafarer*, though they both begin with a set description of the physical hardships of the *wraecca*'s life, and give the traditional heroic answer that they must be overcome by deeds which will win 'a name that shall never die beneath the heavens', are essentially monologues of a new kind. They both take the argument a step further by asking, What if there are no after-livers to keep that name alive? They both give the only positive answer known – the Christian one.

The Wanderer and *The Seafarer*, then, pursue the problem of the *wraecca*'s plight beyond the usual physical and ethical aspects to the threshold of a metaphysical question. This question of the salvation of the individual soul is never so directly asked elsewhere in Anglo–Saxon poetry: to a hitherto unknown extent the authors 'look in their hearts and write'; and the result is an intensity, a desperation quite different from the impersonal sorrow of the heroic poems. But the development of the thought, especially in *The Seafarer*, is ruled by a dialectic which is emotional and does not care for intellectual consistency. Indeed, *The Seafarer* is, in places, self-contradictory; and although such inconsistencies of attitude (towards the sea, in this case) may fairly be explained in dramatic or psychological terms, the practical reason for them, I am sure, is that the oral poet did not have the sustained intellectual control needed to deal with this problem in its new aspect. Another way of putting this would be to say that Christianity had not been fully assimilated into poetic tradition.

The first task of an oral poet was, as we have seen from *Beowulf*, *wordum wrixlan* – to vary the words, wrestle the sense through the lines. It was this that an audience – naturally better able than a reading public to hold a sound in their heads – expected and enjoyed. It was by this management of the sound, of language coming off the tongue, that Shakespeare held his audiences. But Shakespeare's soliloquies also have a sustained build-up of thought which no oral verse can show, and which we have now come to expect and enjoy. Although it must always remain true, as Mallarmé told Degas, that sonnets are written with words, not with ideas, modern verse often relies heavily upon nuances which are intellectual, non-verbal. This is in fact the heritage of three hundred years of classical logic and rhetoric; but also of classical syntax. Anglo-Saxon verse is more paratactical than subordinated. The sense is not marshalled into subordinate and coordinate clauses, it is organized in terms of phrases which can be delivered with attack. The poet had an audience in front of him, not a blank sheet of paper, and he went on adding his sense-sound units until he judged that the point had gone home. In *The Wanderer* and *The Seafarer* there was no traditional theme to adhere to; indeed, the poets had gone beyond the tradition. The unusual number of conjunctions in *The Seafarer* gives the impression that the poet is arguing with himself – a very modern activity for a *scop*.

The abrupt changes of mood and direction in these poems do not in any way diminish their impact or intensity: one does not expect a desperate man to produce a neat 'resolution of theme'. The *angst* of *The Seafarer* shows how far the anonymity of *Widsith* has been left behind; but we must beware of approaching *The Wanderer* and *The Seafarer* with the expectations of a classical and literary tradition. Their eloquence and bleak truth were bred in the school of heroic oral poetry.

A brief account of the structure of *The Wanderer* and *The Seafarer* might be found useful.

THE WANDERER

The Wanderer consists essentially of two speeches linked by a moralizing passage. The first speech is that of a 'home-stepper' (*eardstapa*), a word meaning 'wanderer' or 'grasshopper'. His *wierd* is to roam the seas in search of a lord to replace his dead 'gold-friend'. At verse 29 (in the Anglo-Saxon) he begins to speak of himself in the third person, the better to manage the sorrow he feels when he imagines himself back in the mead-hall. At the end of his speech he reverts to the first person, thinking how, soon or late, the same fate befalls every 'earl'.[3]

The 'bridge passage' begins with some gnomic lines about the folly of boasting. In *Beowulf* the hero boasts in the mead-hall of the deeds he will accomplish; when he has achieved his boast the *scop* celebrates the deed, ensuring that the hero's name will live on among after-speakers. Fame was the immortality of the Northern heroic world. The poet of *The Wanderer* carries the argument a step further by picturing a ruined city in which there are no 'after-speakers'. There is no hint of a redemptive Christian faith: the Maker of men is cast in the role of a Destroyer as inexorable as Wierd itself.

The second speech in *The Wanderer* is that of the wise man, slow to boast, described at the beginning of the link passage. His reflections upon the blasted city whose walls are wrought with the serpent-shapes of destruction offer no consolation: the victory of winter, hail, and night, the agents of Wierd, is complete.

These bleak soliloquies, one autobiographical, the other directed against the world as a whole, together with their linking passage, are set within a more Christian framework by a prologue and an epilogue, both of five lines. In the first one and a half lines of the poem, and again in the last one and a half lines, reference is made to the mercy of God. Some scholars have thought that by putting these Christian quotation marks around the poem the author was trying to expose the hollowness and the hopelessness of the pagan ethic therein expressed. But the very neatness of the parallelism is suspiciously literary, and, to my way of thinking, this interpretation turns the poem inside out. Having made due allowance for the intention of the author, one has to register the impact of the poem itself on one's own consciousness; and to me these genuflexions to the Creator seem somewhat perfunctory. The epilogue, in any case, is written in the metre employed by the religious poets when they are dealing with something of especial solemnity: it has three, not two, stresses in each half-line. It reads very like the postscript of a monastic scribe; and could it be proved that these words formed part of the original poem, we would still have the impression that their author, though he might clearly see the limitations of the heroic ethic, did not have the deeper faith of the author of *The Dream of the Rood*.

THE SEAFARER

Whatever relative weight is attached to the various constituent parts of *The Wanderer* the poem does fall, fairly naturally, into five sections. The structure of *The Seafarer* is less well articulated, and its changes of tack more violent. The poem (by which I mean lines 1–102, concurring in the view that the rest of the text – given here in a prose translation [4] – was a scribal addition) is a soliloquy: a *wraecca* tells of the many winters (years) he has spent in exile on the sea, and the hardships he has borne. His mind then moves (line 33) to the future, and his trepidation at the thought of a new sea-journey he has to make. The manifestations of spring prick him on:

> Cukoo's dirge drags out my heart,
> whets will to the whale's beat
> across wastes of water: far warmer to me
> are the Lord's kindnesses than this life of death
> lent us on land.

This sudden reversal of attitude towards the sea, and the preference expressed for the 'joys of the Lord', as against the fleeting satisfactions of life on land, have made some scholars think that the Seafarer has rejected his previous longing for his old life with lord and kin and is here vowing to devote his life to contemplation, a sea-bound solitary, a pilgrim-hermit of the waves. This theory is much more logical than the poem itself, as any strict line-by-line application of it will show; but the source-diviners and influence-pedlars will not willingly let such a controversy die. More revealing of the haziness in which we all stand as regards these texts is the now discredited theory that *The Seafarer* is a dialogue between an old man and a young man. Only thus could Professor Rieger explain these contradictory attitudes towards the sea.

True it is, in any case, that from this point onwards the persona of the Seafarer is discarded, and the poet launches into a passionate and categorical denial of the permanent value of any human life – except in so far as the individual can overcome his mortality; fame is, according to the traditional formula, earned by deeds 'before wayfaring'. But the deeds this time are against the Devil, and the fame is among the angels.[5] *The Seafarer* then makes its final onslaught: the poet laments the dead lords, the feebleness of their modern successors, the inevitable wasting of our flesh, the futility of hoarding gold if a man's soul is weighed down with sin. This is one of the greatest passages of our literature, and those unsatisfied by my version should look at Ezra Pound's *Seafarer* to see what *le grand translateur* of our age did with it.

A commentary on *The Seafarer* is not called for here. Translation involves as many decisions as there are words in the original – indeed, many more; however inadequate, it is the best critique one can make.

The Wanderer

Who liveth alone longeth for mercy,
Maker's mercy. Though he must traverse
tracts of sea, sick at heart,
– trouble with oars ice-cold waters,
the ways of exile – Wierd is set fast.

Thus spoke such a 'grasshopper', old griefs in his mind,
cold slaughters, the death of dear kinsmen:

'Alone am I driven each day before daybreak
to give my cares utterance.
None are there now among the living
to whom I dare declare me throughly,
tell my heart's thought. Too truly I know
it is in a man no mean virtue
that he keep close his heart's chest,
hold his thought-hoard, think as he may.

No weary mind may stand against Wierd
nor may a wrecked will work new hope;
wherefore, most often, those eager for fame
bind the dark mood fast in their breasts.

So must I also curb my mind,
cut off from country, from kind far distant,
by cares overworn, bind it in fetters;
this since, long ago, the ground's shroud
enwrapped my gold-friend. Wretched I went thence,
winter-wearied, over the waves' bound;
dreary I sought hall of a gold-giver,
where far or near I might find
him who in mead-hall might take heed of me,
furnish comfort to a man friendless,
win me with cheer.
           He knows who makes trial
how harsh and bitter is care for companion

48

to him who hath few friends to shield him.
Track ever taketh him, never the torqued gold,
not earthly glory, but cold heart's cave.
He minds him of hall-men, of treasure-giving,
how in his youth his gold-friend
gave him to feast. Fallen all this joy.

He knows this who is forced to forgo his lord's,
his friend's counsels, to lack them for long:
oft sorrow and sleep, banded together,
come to bind the lone outcast;
he thinks in his heart then that he his lord
claspeth and kisseth, and on knee layeth
hand and head, as he had at otherwhiles
in days now gone, when he enjoyed the gift-stool.

Awakeneth after this friendless man,
seeth before him fallow waves,
seabirds bathing, broading out feathers,
snow and hail swirl, hoar-frost falling.
Then all the heavier his heart's wounds,
sore for his loved lord. Sorrow freshens.

Remembered kinsmen press through his mind;
he singeth out gladly, scanneth eagerly
men from the same hearth. They swim away.
Sailors' ghosts bring not many
known songs there. Care grows fresh
in him who shall send forth too often
over locked waves his weary spirit.

Therefore I may not think, throughout this world,
why cloud cometh not on my mind
when I think over all the life of earls,
how at a stroke they have given up hall,
mood-proud thanes. So this middle earth
each of all days ageth and falleth.'

Wherefore no man grows wise without he have
his share of winters. A wise man holds out;
he is not too hot-hearted, nor too hasty in speech,
nor too weak a warrior, not wanting in fore-thought,
nor too greedy of goods, nor too glad, nor too mild,
nor ever too eager to boast, ere he knows all.

A man should forbear boastmaking
until his fierce mind fully knows
which way his spleen shall expend itself.

A wise man may grasp how ghastly it shall be
when all this world's wealth standeth waste,
even as now, in many places, over the earth
walls stand, wind-beaten,
hung with hoar-frost; ruined habitations.
The wine-halls crumble; their wielders lie
bereft of bliss, the band all fallen
proud by the wall. War took off some,
carried them on their course hence; one a bird bore
over the high sea; one the hoar wolf
dealt to death; one his drear-cheeked
earl stretched in an earthen trench.

The Maker of men hath so marred this dwelling
that human laughter is not heard about it
and idle stand these old giant-works.
A man who on these walls wisely looked
who sounded deeply this dark life
would think back to the blood spilt here,
weigh it in his wit. His word would be this:
'Where is that horse now? Where are those men? Where is
                                        the hoard-sharer?
Where is the house of the feast? Where is the hall's uproar?

        Alas, bright cup! Alas, burnished fighter!
        Alas, proud prince! How that time has passed,
        dark under night's helm, as though it never had been!

50

There stands in the stead of staunch thanes
a towering wall wrought with worm-shapes;
the earls are off-taken by the ash-spear's point,
– that thirsty weapon. Their Wierd is glorious.

Storms break on the stone hillside,
the ground bound by driving sleet,
winter's wrath. Then wanness cometh,
night's shade spreadeth, sendeth from north
the rough hail to harry mankind.

In the earth-realm all is crossed;
Wierd's will changeth the world.
Wealth is lent us, friends are lent us,
man is lent, kin is lent;
all this earth's frame shall stand empty.'

So spoke the sage in his heart; he sat apart in thought.
Good is he who keeps faith: nor should care too fast
be out of a man's breast before he first know the cure:
a warrior fights on bravely. Well is it for him who seeks
                                              forgiveness,
the Heavenly Father's solace, in whom all our fastness stands.

The Seafarer

The tale I frame shall be found to tally:
the history is of myself.
                         Sitting day-long
at an oar's end clenched against clinging sorrow,
breast-drought I have borne, and bitternesses too.
I have coursed my keel through care-halls without end
over furled foam, I forward in the bows
through the narrowing night, numb, watching
for the cliffs we beat along.
                         Cold then
nailed my feet, frost shrank on
its chill clamps, cares sighed
hot about heart, hunger fed
on a mere-wearied mind.
                         No man blessed
with a happy land-life is like to guess
how I, aching-hearted, on ice-cold seas
have wasted whole winters; the wanderer's beat,
cut off from kind. . . .
hung with hoar-frost.
                         Hail flew in showers,
there was no sound there but the slam of waves
along an icy sea. The swan's blare
my seldom amusement; for men's laughter
there was curlew-call, there were the cries of gannets,
for mead-drinking the music of the gull.
To the storm striking the stone cliffs
gull would answer, eagle scream
from throats frost-feathered. No friend or brother
by to speak with the despairing mind.

This he little believes whose life has run
sweet in the burghs, no banished man,
but well-seen at wine-round, my weariness of mind
on the ways stretching over the salt plains.

Night thickened, and from the north snowflakes;
hail fell on the frost-bound earth,
coldest of grains.

> There come thoughts now
knocking my heart, of the high waves,
clashing salt-crests, I am to cross again.
Mind-lust maddens, moves as I breathe
soul to set out, seek out the way
to a far folk-land flood-beyond.

For no man above mould is so mood-proud,
so thoroughly equipped, so quick to do,
so strong in his youth, or with so staunch a lord
that before faring on the sea he does not fear a little
whither the Lord shall lead him in the end.
His heart is not in harping nor in the having of rings,
has no delight in women nor the world's gladnesses
nor can think of any thing outside the thrash of waves,
sea-struck, is distracted, stillness lost.

The thriving of the treeland, the town's briskness,
a lightness over the leas, life gathering,
everything urges the eagerly mooded
man to venture on the voyage he thinks of,
the faring over flood, the far bourn.
And the cuckoo calls him in his care-laden voice,
scout of summer, sings of new griefs
that shall make breast-hoard bitter.

> Blithe heart cannot know,
through its happiness, what hardships they suffer
who drive the foam-furrow furthest from land.
Spirit breaks from the body's chest
to the sea's acres; over earth's breadth
and whale's range roams the mind now,
homes to the breast hungry and thirsty.

Cuckoo's dirge drags out my heart,
whets will to the whale's beat
across wastes of water: far warmer to me
are the Lord's kindnesses than this life of death
lent us on land.

        I do not believe
earthly estate is everlasting:
three things all ways threaten a man's peace
and one before the end shall overthrow his mind;
either illness or age or the edge of vengeance
shall draw out the breath from the doom-shadowed.
Wherefore, for earl whosoever, it is afterword,
the praise of livers-on, that, lasting, is best:
won in the world before wayfaring,
forged, framed here, in the face of enmity,
in the Devil's spite: deeds, achievements.
That after-speakers should respect the name
and after them angels have honour toward it
for always and ever. From those everlasting joys
the daring shall not die.

        Days are soon over,
on earth imperium with the earl's hand fails;
kings are not now, kaisers are not,
there are no gold-givers like the gone masters
who between them framed the first deeds in the world,
in their lives lordly, in the lays renowned.
That chivalry is changed, cheer is gone away,
it is a weaker kind who wields earth now,
sweats for its bread. Brave men are fewer,
all excellence on earth grows old and sere
as now does every man over the world;
age fares against him, his face bleaches
and his thatch thins: had a throng of friends
of noble houses, knows now they all
are given to the ground. That grieves his white head.
Once life is going, this gristle slackens;
nothing can pain or please flesh then,

54

he cannot stir a finger, fix his thinking.
A man may bury his brother with the dead
and strew his grave with the golden things
he would have him take, treasures of all kinds,
but gold hoarded when he here lived
cannot allay the anger of God
towards a soul sin-freighted.

[103-24]

Great is the terrible power of God, before which the earth
shall turn aside; He established the firm foundations, the ex-
panse of the earth, the heavens above. Foolish is the man who
does not fear his Lord; death shall come upon him unprepared.
Blessed is the man who lives in trust; grace shall come to him
from the heavens. The Lord shall confirm that spirit in him,
for he believes in His might. A man should manage a head-
strong spirit and keep it in its place, and be true to men, fair
in his dealings. He should treat every man with measure,
restrain enmity towards friend and foe. He may not wish his
cherished friend to be given over to the fire nor to be burnt
on the pyre, yet Doom is stronger and God is mightier than
any man's conception. Let us think where it is that we may
find a home and then consider how we may come thither,
and then indeed we may strive so that we may be able to
enter into that everlasting blessedness where all life is in the
Lord's love, the bliss of heaven. Thanks be to the Holy One
therefore, the Prince of Glory, the everlasting Lord, that He
has raised us up forever. Amen.

ELEGIES: *THE WIFE'S COMPLAINT*, *THE HUSBAND'S MESSAGE*, *WULF AND EADWACER*

————— *z* —————

The Wife's Complaint and *The Husband's Message* are not separate fragments of a single story, despite what the titles given them by nineteenth-century editors might seem to imply. None of the Elegies give much detail about the situations we are to envisage. Who the characters were, or what exactly has befallen them, are puzzling questions, though, as their editorial history has shown, they are certainly not beyond all conjecture. However, a knowledge of such details is not essential for an appreciation of the poems. The brief introductions given here are really summaries of what can be deduced from internal evidence.

THE WIFE'S COMPLAINT

This is the lament of a woman whose husband, misled by kinsmen, has banished her to an underground den far away from him. Here she recalls their former happiness, curses the author of their estrangement, and pictures her husband stranded on some distant shore.

THE HUSBAND'S MESSAGE

The Husband's Message, which occurs some pages further on in The Exeter Book, is not a particularly elegiac one. The staff upon which the message is carved is made to speak, by a convention which the Riddles will make familiar. The staff tells the lady to whom it has been sent that the signal for her to take ship to rejoin her exiled husband will be the first cry of the cuckoo that she hears. The message ends with the husband's runic signature, for which a proposed solution is given in the Appendix on Runes. Lacunae in the text are the results of the same burn-mark which has disfigured the pages of *The Ruin*.

WULF AND EADWACER

Also in The Exeter Book; this must at first sight have been a very obscure fragment. The chief difficulties were cleared up by Henry Bradley, writing in 1888. He declared that the poem is 'a fragment of a dramatic soliloquy. The speaker, it should be premised, is shown by the grammar to be a woman, Wulf is her lover and an outlaw, and Eadwacer (I suspect, though it is not certain) is her tyrant husband.' The poem is remarkable in that it has a strophic structure (slightly obscured, perhaps in the process of copying), and a refrain. *Deor* is the only other Anglo-Saxon poem similarly constructed.

The Wife's Complaint

I have wrought these words together out of a wryed
                                        existence,
the heart's tally, telling off
the griefs I have undergone from girlhood upwards,
old and new, and now more than ever;
for I have never not had some new sorrow,
some fresh affliction to fight against.

The first was my lord's leaving his people here:
crossed crests. To what country I knew not,
wondered where, awoke unhappy.
I left, fared any road, friendless, an outcast,
sought any service to staunch the lack of him.

Then his kinsmen ganged, began to think
thoughts they did not speak, of splitting the wedlock;
so − estranged, alienated − we lived each
alone, a long way apart; how I longed for him!

In his harshness he had me brought here;
and in these parts there were few friendly-minded,
worth trusting.
                    Trouble in the heart now:
I saw the bitterness, the bound mind
of my matched man, mourning-browed,
mirk in his mood, murder in his thoughts.

Our lips had smiled to swear hourly
that nothing should split us − save dying −
nothing else. All that has changed:
it is now as if it never had been,
our friendship. I feel in the wind
that the man dearest to me detests me.
I was banished to this knoll knotted by woods
to live in a den dug beneath an oak.
Old is this earthen room; it eats at my heart.

I see the thorns thrive up there in thick coverts
on the banks that baulk these black hollows:
not a gay dwelling. Here the grief bred
by lordlack preys on me. Some lovers in this world
live dear to each other, lie warm together
at day's beginning; I go by myself
about these earth caves under the oak tree.
Here I must sit the summer day through,
here weep out the woes of exile,
the hardships heaped upon me. My heart shall never
suddenly sail into slack water,
all the longings of a lifetime answered.

May grief and bitterness blast the mind
of that young man! May his mind ache
behind his smiling face! May a flock of sorrows
choke his chest! He would change his tune
if he lived alone in a land of exile
far from his folk.
                    Where my friend is stranded
frost crusts the cracked cliff-face
grey waves grind the shingle.
The mind cannot bear in such a bleak place
very much grief.
                    He remembers too often
less grim surroundings. Sorrow follows
this too long wait for one who is estranged.

The Husband's Message

Now shall I unseal myself to yourself alone
. . . the wood kind, waxed from saplinghood;
on me . . .   must in foreign lands
set . . .
saltstreams.
                    In the beak of ships
I have often been
where my lord . . .   me
among high houses; and here am come now
on board a ship.
                    You shall directly
know how you may think of the thorough love
my lord feels for you. I have no fear in promising
you shall find him heart-whole, honour bright.

Hwaet!
        The carver of this token entreats a lady
clad in clear stones to call to mind
and hold in her wit words pledged
often between the two in earlier days:
then he would hand you through hall and yard
lord of his lands, and you might live together
forge your love. A feud drove him
from his war-proud people.
                              That prince, glad now,
gave me this word for you: when you shall hear
in the copse at the cliff's edge the cuckoo pitch
his melancholy cry, come over sea.

You will have listened long: leave then with no notice,
let no man alive delay your going:
into the boat and out to sea,
seagull's range; southward from here
over the paths in the foam you shall find your man,
make landfall where your lord is waiting.

He does not conceive, he said to me,
that a greater happiness could be his in this world
than that all-wielding God should grant you both
days when together you may give out rings
among followers and fellows, free-handed deal
the nailed armbands. Of which he has enough,
of inlaid gold . . .

There lands are his, a hearth among strangers,
estate . . .
         . . . of men,
although my lord here . . .
when the need grew strait, steered his boat out
through steep breakers, and had singlehanded
to run the deep ways, dared escape,
mingled saltstreams. The man has now
laid his sorrows, lacks no gladdeners;
he has a hoard and horses and hall-carousing
and would have everything within an earl's having
had he my lady with him: if my lady will come:
if she will hold to what was sworn and sealed in your youths.

So I set together, S and R twinned,
E A, W, D. The oath is named
whereby he undertakes until the end of his life
to keep the covenants of companionship
that, long ago, you delighted to repeat.

Wulf and Eadwacer

The men of my tribe would treat him as game:
if he comes to the camp they will kill him outright.

    Our fate is forked.

Wulf is on one island, I on another.
Mine is a fastness: the fens girdle it
and it is defended by the fiercest men.
If he comes to the camp they will kill him for sure.

    Our fate is forked.

It was rainy weather, and I wept by the hearth,
thinking of my Wulf's far wanderings;
one of the captains caught me in his arms.
It gladdened me then; but it grieved me too.

Wulf, my Wulf, it was wanting you
that made me sick, your seldom coming,
the hollowness at heart; not the hunger I spoke of.

Do you hear, Eadwacer? Our whelp
    Wulf shall take to the wood.
What was never bound is broken easily,
    our song together.

GNOMIC VERSES

———— z ————

THERE is a good deal of popular literature left from Anglo-Saxon times – gnomic verses, charms, riddles, and, in prose, considerable evidence of popular superstitions – but much of it is of curiosity value only and loses little by being read in translation.[1] Here I have translated a sample of the gnomic verses and twenty-nine of the ninety-five riddles in The Exeter Book.

It has been suggested[2] that the collections of gnomic verses in The Exeter Book were authorized by King Alfred. His biographer, Asser, tells us that 'during the frequent wars and other difficulties of this present life, the invasions of the pagans, and his own infirmities of body . . . he continued to recite the Saxon books, and above all to learn by heart the Saxon poems, and to make others learn them'. Alfred translated Boethius and other works from Latin, and had his bishops translate more; there is no reason to suppose that he did not pay the same attention to native tradition.

The gnomic verses, or 'maxims' as they are otherwise called, take the form of generalizations about the natural or the human world. For example:

> Frost shall freeze, fire eat wood

or

> A king shall win a queen with goods;

the 'shall' in these statements includes both 'should' and 'always does': it is the nature of frost to freeze, and kings *do* buy queens with goods.[3] Such observations of the way the world works seem to be of very ancient origin: if any pattern is perceptible in this hotch-potch of saws and sketches, it is that they at once interpret and harmonize human experience of Wierd – the way that things happen; they define the natural order. The lines I have translated open with a celebration of natural forces – Frost, Fire, Earth, and Ice – in which there are vestiges of ritual usage. Woden, the weather-god (better known as the god of battle and death), stands at the head of the genealogies of the house of Wessex, but is not, so far as I know, mentioned in Old English poetry. However, God (the 'One who all can') is still seen as He who 'frees the grain from wonder-lock'.

Gnomic Verses
(lines 71–99)

Frost shall freeze
        fire eat wood
earth shall breed
        ice shall bridge
water a shield wear.
        One shall break
frost's fetters
        free the grain
from wonder-lock
        – One who all can.

Winter shall wane
        fair weather come again
the sun-warmed summer!
        The sound unstill
the deep dead wave
        is darkest longest.
Holly shall to the pyre
        hoard be scattered
when the body's numb.
        Name is best.

A king shall win
        a queen with goods
beakers, bracelets.
        Both must first
be kind with gifts.
        Courage must wax
war-mood in the man,
        the woman grow up
beloved among her people,
        be light of mood
hold close a rune-word
        be roomy-hearted
at hoard-share and horse-giving.

When the hall drinks
she shall always and everywhere
          before any company
greet first
          the father of aethelings
with the first draught
          – deft to his hand she
holds the horn –
          and when they are at home together
know the right way
          to run their household.

The ship must be nailed
          the shield framed
from the light linden.
          But how loving the welcome
of the Frisian wife
          when floats offshore
the keel come home again!
          She calls him within walls,

her own husband
          – hull's at anchor! –
washes salt-stains
          from his stiff shirt
brings out clothes
          clean and fresh
for her lord on land again.
          Love's need is met.

RIDDLES

——— z ———

ARISTOTLE devotes a paragraph of his *Rhetoric* to the riddle, and it is a form found in most ancient literatures, though it has suffered the fate of 'occasional verse' in modern times. The trick, as is well known, is to describe a thing, or, more characteristically, make it speak, in such a way that it is difficult to guess what it is. Today the riddle has been relegated to the Christmas cracker; but the riddles of The Exeter Book are often genuinely enigmatic, and generally less fatuous than the present-day variety.

It will be remembered that in Genesis 'the Lord God, having formed out of the ground all the beasts of the earth and all the fowls of the air brought them to Adam to see what he would call them: for whatsoever Adam called any living creature the same is its name'.[1] This is literally true, for from this primordial Naming all modern nouns and hence the language we speak are descended. Language is the chief means of human communication, and it is the gift of language that distinguishes us from the beasts. The novelty of the riddle is that by making a beast speak or depriving it of its name we render it unrecognizable. The subject of the riddle, animal, vegetable, or mineral, usurps the human prerogative of speech, and, naturally enough, takes a non-human point of view. The effect of this is a dislocation of perspective: a good riddle puzzles and can even be mildly frightening, simply because we do not know what it is that is speaking. The feeling of bafflement grows when we are confronted by a riddle to which no solution has been found. The effect of being asked a riddle by someone who lived eleven hundred years ago is already disconcerting; but not to know the answer is frankly embarrassing. The riddle surprises by presenting the

67

familiar through a non-anthropomorphic lens: the result is strange and beautiful, or delightful, or simply pathetic, but it almost always has the special, rather odd, intensity peculiar to the form.

People in Anglo-Saxon times, living uncomfortably close to the natural world, were well aware that though creation is inarticulate it is animate, and that every created thing, every *wiht*, had its own personality. Though the forces of earth, air, and water were not regularly propitiated or invoked, an awareness of the old methods of sympathetic identification seems to have lingered on, by habit and instinct, in the arts, and certainly in the art of poetry, as is clearly shown by the few charms that remain, corrupt though their texts may be.

The riddle is a sophisticated and harmless form of invocation by imitation: the essence of it is that the poet, by an act of imaginative identification to which Vernon Lee gave the name 'empathy', assumes the personality of some created thing – an animal, a plant, a natural force. Some element of impersonation is involved in any creative act, but by performing this particular ventriloquism the poet extends and diversifies our understanding of – or at least our acquaintance with – the noumenous natural world, of whose life, or even existence, modern men are becoming progressively more unaware. This operation is salutary, and may be said to have a religious value.

The Anglo-Saxon riddles have been almost completely neglected by translators. Mr Peter Whigham pointed out to me that they are perfectly serious poems, and I have found in translating them that thorough-wrought construction and that feeling between delight and horror which qualifies a human product as Art, and not just as evidence for social historians. This does not mean, of course, that the riddles are not funny; they are, on the least generous estimation, more entertaining than the riddle of the Sphinx.

We know next to nothing about The Exeter Book collection of riddles. Riddling was certainly a popular pastime among the Anglo-Saxons, especially in the monasteries, and there are extant collections (in Latin, of course) from the pens of Aldhelm, Bishop of Sherborne, Tatwine, Archbishop of Canterbury, and Eusebius, who was probably Hwaetbert, Abbot of Wearmouth, a friend of Bede. All these draw a good deal on the hundred riddles of Symphosius, a collection perhaps of the fourth century, and all were written in the early eighth century. It is probable that The Exeter Book collection dates from the same time. There is a close similarity between these learned Latin enigmas and some of The Exeter Book collection, but what the exact relationship is it is impossible to tell, since many riddle-subjects are traditional. The provenance and genesis of the collection are unknown, and from internal evidence one can only draw the modest conclusion that the ninety-five riddles were not written by one man. A list of suggested solutions will be found in Appendix B, page 136.

7

When it is earth I tread, make tracks upon water
or keep the houses, hushed is my clothing,
clothing that can hoist me above house-ridges
at times toss me into the tall heaven
where the strong cloud-wind carries me on
over cities and countries; accoutrements that
throb out sound, thrilling strokes
deep-soughing song, as I sail alone
over field and flood, faring on,
resting nowhere. My name is ★ ★ ★ ★.

9

Abandoned unborn by my begetters
I was still dead a few spring days ago:
no beat in the breast, no breath in me.

A kinswoman covered me in the clothes she wore,
no kind but kind indeed. I was coddled and swaddled
as close as I had been a baby of her own,
until, as had been shaped, so shielded, though no kin,
the unguessed guest grew great with life.

She fended for me, fostered me, she fed me up,
till I was of a size to set my bounds
further afield. She had fewer dear
sons and daughters because she did so.

12

While my ghost lives I go on feet,
rend the ground, green leas.

When breath is gone I bind the hands
of swart Welsh; worthier men, too.

I may be a bottle: bold warrior
swigs from my belly.
                    Or a bride may set
proudly her foot on me.
                    Or, far from her Wales,
a dark-headed girl grabs and squeezes me,
silly with drink, and in the dark night
wets me with water, or warms me up
before the fire. Fetched between breasts
by her hot hand, while she heaves about
I must stroke her swart part.
                    Say my name:
who living live off the land's wealth
and, when dead, drudge for men.

25

I'm the world's wonder, for I make women happy
– a boon to the neighbourhood, a bane to no one,
though I may perhaps prick the one who picks me.

I am set well up, stand in a bed,
have a roughish root. Rarely (though it happens)
a churl's daughter more daring than the rest
– and lovelier! – lays hold of me,
rushes my red top, wrenches at my head,
and lays me in the larder.
                    She learns soon enough,
the curly-haired creature who clamps me so,
of my meeting with her: moist is her eye!

26

I am the scalp of myself, skinned by my foeman:
robbed of my strength, he steeped and soaked me,
dipped me in water, whipped me out again,
set me in the sun. I soon lost there
the hairs I had had.
                              The hard edge
of a keen-ground knife cuts me now,
fingers fold me, and a fowl's pride
drives its treasure trail across me,
bounds again over the brown rim,
sucks the wood-dye, steps again on me,
makes his black marks.
                                        A man then hides me
between stout shield-boards stretched with hide,
fits me with gold. There glows on me
the jewelsmith's handiwork held with wires.

Let these royal enrichments and this red dye
and splendid settings spread the glory
of the Protector of peoples – and not plague the fool.
If the sons of men will make use of me
they shall be the safer and the surer of victory,
the wiser in soul, the sounder in heart,
the happier in mind. They shall have the more friends,
loving and kinsmanlike, kind and loyal,
good ones and true, who will gladly increase
their honour and happiness, and, heaping upon them
graces and blessings, in the embraces of love
will clasp them firmly. Find out how I am called,
my celebrated name, who in myself am holy,
am of such service, and salutary to men.

27

Men are fond of me. I am found everywhere,
brought in from the woods and the beetling cliffs,
from down and from dale. In the daylight wings
raised me aloft, then into a roof's shade
swung me in sweetly. Sweltered then
by men in a bath, I am a binder now,
soon a thrasher, a thrower next:
I'll put an old fellow flat on the ground.
A man who tries to take me on,
tests my strength, soon finds out,
if his silly plan doesn't pall on him,
that it is his back that will hit the dust.
Loud in words, he has lost control
of his hands and feet, and his head doesn't work:
his strength has gone. Guess my name
who have such mastery of men on earth
that I knock them about in broad daylight.

29

A curious and wonderful creature I saw,
– bright air-grail, brave artefact –
homing from a raid with its haul of silver
brimming precarious crescent horns.

To build itself a hideaway high up in the city,
a room in a tower, timbered with art,
was all it aimed at, if only it might.

Then over the wall rose a wonder familiar
to the earth-race, to everyone known.
It gathered to itself the hoard, and to its home drove off
that unhappy outcast. Onward it coursed,
wandered westward with wasting heart.

Dust rose to the skies, dew fell to the earth,
night was no more. No man knew
along what ways it wandered after.

30

I am fire-fretted and I flirt with Wind
and my limbs are light-freighted and I am lapped in flame
and I am storm-stacked and I strain to fly
and I am a grove leaf-bearing and a glowing ember.

From hand to friend's hand about the hall I go,
so much do lords and ladies love to kiss me.
When I hold myself high, and the whole company
bow quiet before me, their blessedness
shall flourish skyward beneath my fostering shade.

33

Strange the creature that stole through the water.
Grandly she called from her keel to the land,
lifted her loud voice. Her laughter was fearful,
awful where it was known; her edges sharp.
Slow to enter, she was not slack in battle;
hard, and, in deeds of destruction, unyielding:
she crushed wooden walls. Wicked the spell
that she cunningly unbound about her creation:
'My mother – and I am the most daring
of all the sex – is also my daughter
when grown up in strength. It is granted likewise
by the wise among the people, that in every part of the earth,
in whatever station, she stands gracefully.'

34

She feeds the cattle, this creature I have seen
in the houses of men. Many are her teeth
and her nose is of service to her. Netherward she goes,
loyally plundering and pulling home again;

she hunts about the walls in hope of plants,
finding always some that are not firmly set.
She leaves the fair fast-rooted ones
to stand undisturbed in their established place,
brightly shining, blossoming and growing.

35

The womb of the wold, wet and cold,
bore me at first, brought me forth.
I know in my mind my making was not
through skill with fells or fleeces of wool;
there was no winding of wefts, there is no woof in me,
no thread thrumming under the thrash of strokes,
no whirring shuttle steered through me,
no weaver's reed rapped my sides.
The worms that braid the broidered silk
with Wierd cunning did not weave me;
yet anywhere over the earth's breadth
men will attest me a trustworthy garment.

Say truly, supple-minded man,
wise in words, what my name is.

38

I watched a beast of the weaponed sex.
He forced, fired by the first of lusts,
four fountains which refreshed his youth
to shoot out shining in their shaped ways.

A man stood by that said to me:
'That beast, living, will break clods;
torn to tatters, will tie men's hands.'

42

I saw two wonderful and weird creatures
out in the open unashamedly
fall a–coupling. If the fit worked,
the proud blonde in her furbelows got
what fills women.
        The floor's my table:
the runes I trace tell any man
acquainted with books both the creatures'
names in one.
      Need (N) shall be there
twice over; two Oaks (A);
and the bright Ash (Æ) – one only in the line –
and Hail (H) twice too.
        Who the hoard's door
with a key's power can unlock
that guards the riddle against rune-guessers,
holds its heart close, hides it loyally
with cunning bonds?
        Clear now
to men at wine by what names
this shameless couple are called among us.

43

I know of one who is noble and brave,
a guest in our courts. Neither grim hunger
nor hot thirst can harm him at all,
neither age nor illness. If only the servant
whom on his journey he has to have with him
serves him faithfully, they shall find appointed,
when safe in their homeland, happiness and feasting,
untold bliss – but bitterness otherwise,
if the lord's servant serves his master
ill on the way. One must not be

a burden to his brother or both will suffer
when they are jointly drawn on their journey elsewhere
and must leave the company of the kinswoman who is
their only sister and their mother. Let the man who will,
declare graciously how the guest might be called,
or else the servant, whom I speak of here.

44

Swings by his thigh a thing most magical!
Below the belt, beneath the folds
of his clothes it hangs, a hole in its front end,
stiff-set and stout, but swivels about.

Levelling the head of this hanging instrument,
its wielder hoists his hem above the knee:
it is his will to fill a well-known hole
that it fits fully when at full length.

He has often filled it before. Now he fills it again.

47

I heard of a wonder, of words moth-eaten;
that is a strange thing, I thought, weird
that a man's song be swallowed by a worm,
his binded sentences, his bedside stand-by
rustled in the night – and the robber-guest
not one whit the wiser for the words he had mumbled.

50

There is on earth a warrior wonderfully engendered:
between two dumb creatures it is drawn into brightness
for the use of men. Meaning harm, a foe

bears it against his foe. Fierce in its strength,
a woman may tame it. Well will he heed
and meekly serve both men and women
if they have the trick of tending him,
and feed him properly. He promotes their happiness,
enhances their lives. Allowed to become
proud, however, he proves ungrateful.

51

I saw four fine creatures
travelling in company; their tracks were dark,
their trail very black. The bird that floats
in the air swoops less swiftly than their leader;
he dived beneath the wave. Drudgery was it
for the fellow that taught all four of them their ways
on their ceaseless visits to the vessel of gold.

57

Their dark bodies, dun-coated,
when the breeze bears them up over the backs of the hills
are black, diminutive.
     Bold singers,
they go in companies, call out loudly;
they tread the timbered cliff, and at times the eaves
of men's houses.
     How do they call themselves?

60

I was by the sand at the sea-wall once:
where the tide comes I kept my dwelling,
fast in my first seat. There were few indeed

of human kind who cared to behold
my homeland in that lonely place,
but in every dawning the dark wave
lapped about me. Little did I think
that early or late I ever should
speak across the meadbench, mouthless as I am,
compose a message. It is a mysterious thing,
dark to the mind that does not know,
how a knife's point and a clever hand,
a man's purpose and a point also,
have pressed upon me to the purpose that
I might fearlessly announce, for none but us two,
a message to you, so that no man beside
might spread abroad what is spoken between us.

68

The wave, over the wave, a wierd thing I saw,
thorough-wrought, and wonderfully ornate:
a wonder on the wave – water become bone.

69

The thing is magic, unimaginable
to him who knows not how it is.
It throstles through its sides, its throat angled
and turned with knowledge, two barrels
set sharp on the shoulder.
                          Its shaping is fulfilled
as it stands by the wayside so wonderful to see,
tall and gleaming, to glad the passer-by.

73

I was a pure girl and a grey-maned woman
and, at the same time, a singular man.
I flew with the birds, breasted the sea,
sank beneath the wave, dissolved among fish
and alighted on land. I had a living soul.

75

I saw a lady sit alone.

76

I fed in the deep folds of the sea:
waves covered me, close to the land.
Often to the ocean I opened my mouth:
foot had I none. Now my flesh will be
meat for a man. He'll not mind my outside
once his knife's sharpness has sheared a way
between me and my hide. Hastily then
he'll eat me, uncooked . . .

79

Hwaet!
    I am always at the aetheling's shoulder,
his battle-fellow, bound to him in love.
I follow the king. Flaxen-headed
lady may lay her light hand on me,
though she be of clearest blood, an earl's child.
I hold in my heart the hollow tree's fruit,
ride out in front on a fierce steed
when the host goes harrying, harsh-tongued then,

bear to songsmith when singing's done
his word-won gift. I have a good nature,
and in myself am swart. Say what I am called.

80

I am puff-breasted, proud-crested,
a head I have, and a high tail,
eyes and ears and one foot,
both my sides, a back that's hollow,
a very stout beak, a steeple neck
and a home above men.
                              Harsh are my sufferings
when that which makes the forest tremble takes and shakes
                                                            me.

Here I stand under streaming rain
and blinding sleet, stoned by hail;
freezes the frost and falls the snow
on me stuck-bellied. And I stick it all out
for I cannot change the chance that made me.

84

My home is not silent: I myself am not loud.
The Lord has provided for the pair of us
a joint expedition. I am speedier than he
and sometimes stronger; he stays the course better.
Sometimes I rest, but he runs on.
For as long as I live I live in him;
if we leave one another it is I who must die.

85

Many were met, men of discretion
wisdom and wit, when in there walked. . . .

Two ears it had, and one eye solo,
two feet and twelve hundred heads,
back, belly, a brace of hands,
a pair of sides and shoulders and arms
and one neck. Name, please.

THE DREAM OF THE ROOD

—————— z ——————

The Dream of the Rood, as it is Gothically called, was a famous poem in its own day, and its history is not without interest. The first record of it that we have are lines carved in runic characters on the huge cross which stands in the chancel of the kirk at Ruthwell, Dumfriesshire. This six-metre-high rood, perhaps the most famous single Anglo-Saxon monument, is covered with scenes in relief and runic inscriptions in the Northumbrian dialect. It was made soon after the return from Rome of Coelfrith, Abbot of Wearmouth and Jarrow; when the abbot was in the Holy City, Pope Sergius I had discovered a fragment of the True Cross. This was in the year 701.

In 884 Pope Marinus sent Alfred another piece of the True Cross, and expanded versions of *The Dream of the Rood* were made, one of which is in the Vercelli Book, a manuscript written perhaps ninety years later, now in the library of the Cathedral of St Andrew at Vercelli, a station on the English route to Rome.

Soon afterwards Aethelmaer, a member of the royal house of Wessex, founder of Cerne Abbas and Eynsham, patron of Aelfric ('the father of English prose') and heir of Ealdorman Bryhtnoth, the leader of the East Saxons at the battle of Maldon, had a reliquary made to hold Alfred's fragment – now the largest piece of the True Cross in existence. This silver reliquary, known as the Brussels Cross, has a quotation from *The Dream of the Rood* inscribed upon it.

The only complete text of the poem is the one in the Vercelli Book; I have translated into verse lines 1–77 of this version, concurring in the old opinion that the text is not only expanded but composite, and that the latter half, from a different hand, is inferior; I give it in a literal prose version.

It is a testimony both to the unity of Christendom and the breadth of an oral tradition that the most famous of Old English religious poems, composed to celebrate the finding of a piece of the True Cross, should today be preserved in three different (but from the point of view of an oral tradition equally 'authoritative') forms, inscribed by hand in stone, on skin, and in silver, written in three different dialects of English, each version in a different century, and, finally, that none of them should happen to be in England today.

The Dream of the Rood is unique perhaps in the literature of the world, certainly in that of Anglo-Saxon England. Most of the Old English religious verse consists of paraphrases of the Vulgate or of Latin Saints' Lives. The material of the sacred stories was not easily assimilable into Germanic tradition, and the old poets found some things frankly intractable. Consequently the poems are all very uneven, veering between uncomprehending awe and pagan enthusiasm. The Old Testament, with its fierce tribalism, its jealous God and its acceptance of the duty of vengeance, was more congenial to the *scop* than the New, and the themes of the Pentateuch came easily to him. The Anglo-Saxon *Genesis*, for example, sees Satan as a man disloyal to his lord – one of the key situations in all Germanic poetry – and makes his speeches at least as dramatic and defiant as those of Milton's Satan. And there are equally successful passages in the other narrative poems where the poet has managed to interpret a Judaic in terms of a Germanic theme; but these passages must be counted as exceptions. Old English religious verse has an unpredictability and fascination all of its own, partly because it is so different from the more familiar Christian verse of the latter Middle Ages and it is rarely as insipid as modern devotional verse; but it is at times clumsy, rambling, and uncertain of itself. It also seems less Christian than many of its partisans (apparently quite innocent of comparative mythology) would have one believe, and the poems are very dubious evidence of a rapid and complete conversion of the English. The significance of the incarnation, life, death, and resurrection of Christ is not often properly realized in Old English verse.

To these bald generalizations *The Dream of the Rood* is an exception on every count. It is a brief description of an orthodox mystical experience, and its author is perfectly in command of his material. He tells us how the Rood appeared to him, and of the words it spoke. The vision is thus expressed in a way natural to the *scop* and to his audience – that is, in the form of a riddle, or rather of the two most typical riddle-forms combined: the 'I saw' type plus the 'I am' type. This conception is little short of a stroke of genius, and lends the words of the Cross a wonderful dramatic intensity and freshness. The idea of making the Cross speak is not unparalleled (see Riddle 30, last sentence), and there is certainly much evidence that the author knew the Passiontide liturgy well; but nothing can detract from the originality of putting the most dramatic and most revered of Christian themes into a pagan form traditionally reserved for party games. The Christian wine shines in the pagan bottle with a new light.

A note may be necessary on the occurrence of the longer six-stress line in *The Dream of the Rood*; it seems to be used at particularly solemn moments.

The poem has been well edited by Michael Swanton, who places it in its proper doctrinal, cultural and artistic context.

The Dream of the Rood

Hwaet!
A dream came to me
     at deep midnight
when humankind
     kept their beds
— the dream of dreams!
     I shall declare it.

It seemed I saw the Tree itself
borne on the air, light wound about it,
— a beam of brightest wood, a beacon clad
in overlapping gold, glancing gems
fair at its foot, and five stones
set in a crux flashed from the crosstree.

Around angels of God
    all gazed upon it,
since first fashioning fair.
    It was not a felon's gallows,
for holy ghosts beheld it there,
and men on mould, and the whole Making shone for it
— *signum* of victory!
              Stained and marred,
stricken with shame, I saw the glory-tree
shine out gaily, sheathed in yellow
decorous gold; and gemstones made
for their Maker's Tree a right mail-coat.

Yet through the masking gold I might perceive
what terrible sufferings were once sustained thereon:
it bled from the right side.
    Ruth in the heart.

Afraid I saw that unstill brightness
change raiment and colour
    — again clad in gold
or again slicked with sweat,

spangled with spilling blood.

Yet lying there a long while
I beheld, sorrowing, the Healer's Tree
till it seemed that I heard how it broke silence,
best of wood, and began to speak:

'Over that long remove my mind ranges
back to the holt where I was hewn down;
from my own stem I was struck away,
    dragged off by strong enemies,
wrought into a roadside scaffold.
    They made me a hoist for wrongdoers.

The soldiers on their shoulders bore me,
    until on a hill-top they set me up;
many enemies made me fast there.
    Then I saw, marching toward me,
mankind's brave King;
    He came to climb upon me.

I dared not break or bend aside
against God's will, though the ground itself
shook at my feet. Fast I stood,
who falling could have felled them all.

Almighty God ungirded Him,
    eager to mount the gallows,
unafraid in the sight of many:
    He would set free mankind.
I shook when His arms embraced me
    but I durst not bow to ground,
stoop to Earth's surface.
    Stand fast I must.

I was reared up, a rood.
    I raised the great King,
liege lord of the heavens,
    dared not lean from the true.

They drove me through with dark nails:
   on me are the deep wounds manifest,
wide-mouthed hate-dents.
     I durst not harm any of them.
How they mocked at us both!
     I was all moist with blood
sprung from the Man's side
     after He sent forth His soul.

Wry wierds a-many I underwent
up on that hill-top; saw the Lord of Hosts
stretched out stark. Darkness shrouded
the King's corse. Clouds wrapped
its clear shining. A shade went out
wan under cloud-pall. All creation wept,
keened the King's death. Christ was on the Cross.

But there quickly came from far
earls to the One there. All that I beheld;
had grown weak with grief,
     yet with glad will bent then
meek to those men's hands,
     yielded Almighty God.

They lifted Him down from the leaden pain,
     left me, the commanders,
standing in a sweat of blood.
     I was all wounded with shafts.

They straightened out His strained limbs,
     stood at His body's head,
looked down on the Lord of Heaven
     – for a while He lay there resting –
set to contrive Him a tomb
     in the sight of the Tree of Death,
carved it of bright stone,
     laid in it the Bringer of Victory,
spent from the great struggle.
     They began to speak the grief-song,

sad in the sinking light,
        then thought to set out homeward;
their hearts were sick to death,
        their most high Prince
they left to rest there with scant retinue.

Yet we three, weeping, a good while
stood in that place after the song had gone up
from the captains' throats. Cold grew the corse,
fair soul-house.
                They felled us all.
We crashed to ground, cruel Wierd,
and they delved for us a deep pit.

The Lord's men learnt of it,
His friends found me . . .
it was they who girt me with gold and silver . . .

[78–156]

'Now, my dear man, you may understand that I have suffered to the end the pain of grievous sorrows at the hands of dwellers in misery. The time is now come that men on earth, and all this marvellous creation, shall honour me far and wide and address themselves in prayer to this sign. On me the Son of God spent a time of suffering. Therefore do I now tower up glorious beneath the heavens, and I have the power to save every man who fears me. Formerly I was made the worst of punishments, the most hateful to the peoples – before I opened to men, the speech-bearers, the right way to life.

Behold, the Prince of Glory then exalted me above the trees of the forest, the Keeper of the Kingdom of Heaven; just as He also, Almighty God, for the sake of all mankind, exalted His mother, Mary herself, above all womankind.

I now command you, my dear man, to tell men about this sight, reveal in words that this is the tree of glory on which Almighty God suffered for the many sins of mankind and Adam's deeds of old. He tasted death thereupon; yet afterwards the Lord rose up, to help men with His great might. Then He went up to the heavens. Hither He shall come again to seek out mankind on the day of doom, the Lord Himself, Almighty God, and with Him His angels, when He then will adjudge – Who has the power of judgement – to each and every one according to how he shall formerly have deserved for himself here in this transitory life. Nor can anyone there be unconcerned about the word that the Ruler shall utter. He shall ask before the multitude, Where is the man who is willing to taste bitter death for the Lord's name's sake? – as He had formerly done on the tree. But they shall then be afraid, and few shall think what they shall begin to answer to Christ. Yet no one there shall need to be afraid who has borne in his bosom the best of signs. But every soul on earth who intends to dwell with the Lord shall come to the Kingdom through the Rood.'

Then I prayed to the tree with cheerful heart and high zeal, alone as I was and with small retinue. My spirit was drawn forth on its way hence; in all it had endured many times of longing. The hope of my life is now that I should seek out that tree of victory, alone and more frequently than all men, to worship it fully. The desire to do this is strong in my mind, and my hope of protection is all bent on the rood. I have not many powerful friends on earth. On the contrary, they have departed hence out of the world's joys, have sought out the King of Glory and live now in the heavens with the Almighty Father, dwelling in glory; and every day I look for the time when the Lord's rood, which once I gazed on here on earth, shall fetch me forth from this fleeting life and then shall bring me where there is great rejoicing, happiness in the heavens, where the Lord's people is seated at the feast, where there is bliss everlasting; and then He shall appoint me to a place where after I may dwell in glory, and fully share in joy among the blest.

May the Lord be my friend, who here on earth once suffered on the gallows tree for the sins of man. He ransomed us and gave us life, a heavenly home. Hope was made new, with glory and with bliss, for those who had suffered burning there. The Son was victorious on that expedition,★ mighty and triumphant, when He came, the Almighty Sovereign, with a multitude, a host of spirits, into God's Kingdom, to the bliss of the angels and all of the saints who had previously dwelt in glory, when their Ruler came, Almighty God, into His own Kingdom.

★ The Harrowing of Hell

THE PHOENIX

――――― z ―――――

The Phoenix is an anonymous expansion of *De Phoenice*, an exotic poem sometimes attributed to the Latin Christian writer of the fourth century, Lactantius. The Old English tenth-century adaptation continues by adding a commentary based upon a Latin commentary by St Ambrose. *The Phoenix* is an allegorization of the life, death and rebirth of the fabulous oriental bird as a type of Christ's resurrection. I have translated the unusually sensuous initial description of the bird and of the paradisal land where it dwells.

From *The Phoenix*
(lines 71-89)

The groves are hung with growing fruit,
bright to look upon; the burden of those woods
favoured by heaven does not fail ever.
Nor does blossom, the beauty of trees,
lie waste upon the ground; wonderfully rather,
the branches of the trees bear always
perpetual plenty of fruit
and stand out green above the grassy plain.
It is the most glorious of groves, its gay adornment
the work of the Holy One. The woods' canopy
is not to be broken, and it breathes out incense
through that happy land. This shall last unchanging
for ever and ever, until the Ancient One
shall ordain an end to all He first created.

Beautiful is the bird abiding in that wood,
fair and feathered strongly: Phoenix is his name.
There he lives alone, looking out upon his homeland;
dauntless he surveys it. Death shall not touch him
on that lovely plain, for as long as the world lasts.

BRUNANBURH

———— *z* ————

Brunanburh is a celebration of the great victory won by Wessex over its enemies in 937, and is the first poem to appear in the Anglo-Saxon Chronicle. King Athelstan and his brother Edmund, with Mercian help, defeated a combined invading force of Scots, Picts, Strathclyde British and the formidable Dublin-based Vikings at a place called Brunanburh, which cannot now be identified. It was one of the first great *English* victories; its patriotic appeal may have recommended it to Tennyson, for it is the only Old English poem he chose to translate.

In *Brunanburh* the old oral-formulaic poetry is put to new purposes: among what survives, it is the first royal panegyric, the first court poem, the first heroic poem to mention historiography and the reading of books, and the last piece of correct versification in Old English. It is an anthology of all the proper devices of the old battle poetry, but it is also the last battle poem.

Brunanburh

Athelstan the King, captain of men,
ring-giver of warriors − and with him his brother
Edmund the Atheling − unending glory
won in that strife by their swords' edges
that there was about Brunanburh. The board-wall they cut
through,

cleft the lindens with the leavings of hammers,
Edward's offspring, answering the blood
they had from their forebears: that in the field they should
often

against every foe defend the land,
hoard and homes. The hated ones fell,
the people of the Scots and the shipmen too,
fell as was fated. The field was running
with the blood of soldiers from the sun's rise
at the hour of the morning when that marvellous star,
God's bright candle, glided over the lands,
to the time when the creature of the eternal Lord
sank to rest. Then sated with battle
and weary lay many there, men of the Northerners
shot above their shields, and Scots men likewise,
wasted by spears. The West Saxons
rode in troop right through the day
hard on the heels of the hated peoples,
pursuing hewed fiercely at the fleeing warriors
with mill-sharpened swords. The Mercians did not refuse
the hard hand-play to any hero among those
who with Anlaf over the ocean's courses
in the bosom of a ship had sought our land
and their doom in that fight. There were five kings
who in their youth lay low on that battlefield,
slain by the sword; and seven earls
of Anlaf's also; others without number
of shipmen and Scots. With scant retinue
the prince of the Northmen was put to flight

by stark need to the stern of his craft:
the long ship drove out across the dark waters;
the king slipped away, saved his life.
The old king likewise came away also,
the grey-haired campaigner, Constantine, fled
to the North he knew. He had no need to rejoice
in that meeting of swords where he was shortened of kinsmen
and deprived of friends on the field of assembly,
plucked on the battlefield: on that place of slaughter
he left his son brought low by wounds,
young on the battlefield. The yield of the swords
gave no ground for boasting to the grey-haired chieftain,
the old enemy; to Anlaf neither.
They had no cause to laugh with those left from the war,
that they had been the better in battle-accomplishment
on the field of strife when the standards clashed,
at the spear-meeting when men came together
in the exchange of weapons: when with Edward's sons
they had played together in the place of slaughter.

    The nailed ships of the Norsemen took off
what spears had spared, a spattered remnant,
across deep Dingsmere to Dublin once more,
to seek again Ireland in shame.
The brothers also, both of them together,
the King and the Atheling, came away to their own,
the West-Saxon land, in war-triumph.
The corpse-sharers, shadowy-coated,
they left behind them: the black raven
with its horny beak; the brown eagle
of white tail-feather, to feast on the slain
– greedy war-hawk; and the grey one,
the wolf of the weald.

        No worse slaughter
in this island has ever yet
before these days befallen a people
by the edge of the sword – so say the books,
the wise men of old – since from the East came

Angles and Saxons up to these shores,
seeking Britain across the broad seas,
smart for glory, those smiths of war
that overcame the Welsh, and won a homeland.

THE BATTLE OF MALDON

—————— z ——————

The entry for the year 991 in the Anglo-Saxon Chronicle begins as follows:

In this year Anlaf came with ninety-three ships to Folkestone and ravaged the neighbourhood, went on to Sandwich, and thence to Ipswich, and overran the whole area, and so to Maldon. And there Ealdorman Bryhtnoth and his *fyrd* came to meet him, and fought with him. And they killed the Ealdorman and the battlefield was theirs. . . .

Another version of the Chronicle adds that the tribute paid after the English defeat was as much as *x thusend punda*.

In the reign of Aethelred 'the Unready' such Danish raids were an annual occurrence, and Maldon, though not an 'important' battle, must have been a typical one. The Viking leader, Anlaf, may possibly be Olaf Tryggvason, later King of Norway and the hero of a saga; Bryhtnoth, Ealdorman of Essex, was one of the four or five greatest men in England. The battle is recorded elsewhere in later Latin histories by monks of Ely and Ramsey, two houses toward which Bryhtnoth showed favour; but the fullest, soberest and most authoritative account is to be found in the 325 verses of *The Battle of Maldon*. The author obviously knew the men and the place concerned, and may well have been a participant. His tone is aristocratic; there is no reason to suppose that he was not a member of the Earl's *comitatus* of hearth- and shoulder-companions.

The names of Bryhtnoth's followers and the topography of the battle are the only confusing features of what is otherwise a very straightforward story. Several of the heroes of the series of individual combats in which the battle is

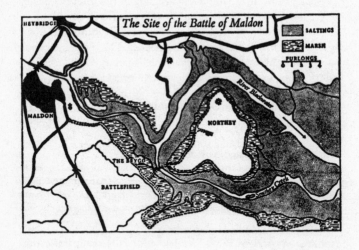

The Site of the Battle of Maldon

conventionally described are historically identifiable, and they will all be found in the Glossary of Proper Names. The problem of the exact site of the battle has been cleared up by E. D. Laborde. The Danes (a name given to all Scandinavians) sailed up the estuary of the River Pant, or Blackwater, and beached their ships on Northey Island (see map). The Blackwater Estuary is tidal, and the shallows would have been dangerous for the ships; besides, islands were often chosen by the Vikings as a good base, providing shelter if the need for a quick getaway arose. But Northey Island is linked to the mainland only by a causeway eighty yards long and eight feet wide, and Bryhtnoth had drawn up the *fyrd* of Essex at the far end. When the Vikings' demand for tribute was refused, they tried to come across the 'bridge' (as it is called in the poem) as soon as the tide would allow. But the Norsemen presented an easy target for the spears of the East Saxons, and there would have been no Battle of Maldon had not Bryhtnoth decided *for his ofermode* to allow the Danish request to come across the ford unmolested and form their shield-wall on dry land again.

This act of rash magnanimity was made in the interests of fair play; but the English were up against professionals. Leading the attack against the heathen, the elderly Bryhtnoth was cut down, and many of his followers fled. The Earl's personal retinue fought to the bitter end, encouraging each other by exhortation and example. The poem breaks off soon after Bryhtwold, a man who has grown old in the service of the Earl, has spoken these words, which have often, and rightly, been taken as the classic declaration of the heroic faith:

> Thought shall be the harder, heart the keener,
> mood the more, as our might lessens.

Maldon is remarkable (apart from the fact that it is a master-piece) in that it shows that the strongest motive in a Germanic society, still, nine hundred years after Tacitus, was an absolute and overriding loyalty to one's lord. The heroic ethic is presented in *Maldon* in all its integrity: in these unpretentious, still-regular verses it receives its clearest and most convincing expression. *Maldon* is without doubt the finest battle-poem in English, not because of any particular vividness of description (though that is not absent), but because the anonymous author, deeply committed to the cause of these particular English Christian men, who were his friends, and uninfluenced by any literary ideal of courage, presents what he saw in the tradi-tional way, ruthlessly subordinating everything to the unity and truth of his account. As a work of art, *The Battle of Maldon* is certainly, within its narrower terms of reference, a better poem than *Beowulf*.

The original eleventh-century Worcester MS, which also contained Asser's *Life of Alfred*, was burnt in the fire at Sir Robert Cotton's library in 1731. With it perished a tantalizing work entitled *The Passion of the 11000 Virgins*. Fortunately, the underkeeper of the library, John Elphinston, had made a copy of *Maldon*, from which Thomas Hearne (Pope's Wormius) prepared an edition; these are all we now have. Before the copy was made leaves had been lost from the MS, and the beginning and the end of the poem are lost.

The Battle of Maldon

. . . would be broken.

Then he bade each man let go bridles
drive far the horses and fare forward,
fit thought to hand-work and heart to fighting.

Whereat one of Offa's kin, knowing the Earl
would not suffer slack-heartedness,
loosed from his wrist his loved hawk;
over the wood it stooped: he stepped to battle.
By that a man might know this young man's will
to weaken not at the war-play: he had taken up weapons.

Eadric also would serve the Earl,
his lord, in the fight. He went forth
with spear to battle, his spirit failed not
while he with hand might yet hold
board and broadsword: he made good his boast
to stand fast in fight before his lord.

Then Bryhtnoth dressed his band of warriors,
from horseback taught each man his task,
where he should stand, how keep his station.
He bade them brace their linden-boards aright,
fast in finger-grip, and to fear not.
Then when his folk was fairly ranked
Bryhtnoth alighted where he loved best to be
and was held most at heart – among hearth-companions.

Then stood on strand and called out sternly
a Viking spokesman. He made speech –
threat in his throat, threw across the seamen's
errand to the Earl where he stood on our shore.

'The swift-striking seafarers send me to thee,
bid me say that thou send for thy safety
rings, bracelets. Better for you
that you stay straightaway our onslaught with tribute

than that we should share bitter strife.
We need not meet if you can meet our needs:
for a gold tribute a truce is struck.

Art captain here: if thou tak'st this course,
art willing to pay thy people's ransom,
wilt render to Vikings what they think right,
buying our peace at our price,
we shall with that tribute turn back to ship,
fare out on the flood, and hold you as friends.'

Bryhtnoth spoke. He raised shield-board,
shook the slim ash-spear, shaped his words.
Stiff with anger, he gave him answer:

'Hearest 'ou, seaman, what this folk sayeth?
Spears shall be all the tribute they send you,
viper-stained spears and the swords of forebears,
such a haul of harness as shall hardly profit you.

Spokesman for scavengers, go speak this back again,
bear your tribe a bitterer tale:
that there stands here 'mid his men not the meanest of Earls,
pledged to fight in this land's defence,
the land of Aethelred, my liege lord,
its soil, its folk. In this fight the heathen
shall fall. It would be a shame for your trouble
if you should with our silver away to ship
without fight offered. It is a fair step hither:
you have come a long way into our land.

But English silver is not so softly won:
first iron and edge shall make arbitrement,
harsh war-trial, ere we yield tribute.'

He bade his brave men bear their shields forward
until they all stood at the stream's edge,
though they might not clash yet for the cleaving waters.
After the ebb the flood came flowing in;
the sea's arms locked. Overlong it seemed

before they might bear spear-shafts in shock together.
So they stood by Panta's stream in proud array,
the ranks of the East Saxons and the host from the ash-ships,
nor might any of them harm another
save who through arrow-flight fell dead.

The flood went out. Eager the fleet-men stood,
the crowding raiders, ravening for battle;
then the heroes' Helm bade hold the causeway
a war-hard warrior – Wulfstan was his name –
come of brave kin. It was this Ceola's son
who with his Frankish spear struck down the first man there
as he so boldly stepped onto the bridge's stonework.

There stood with Wulfstan staunch warriors,
Aelfhere and Maccus, men of spirit
who would not take flight from the ford's neck
but fast defence make against the foemen
the while that they might wield their weapons.
When the hated strangers saw and understood
what bitter bridge-warders were brought against them there,
they began to plead with craft, craving leave
to fare over the ford and lead across their footmen.

Then the Earl was overswayed by his heart's arrogance
to allow overmuch land to that loath nation:
the men stood silent as Brighthelm's son
called out over the cold water.

   'The ground is cleared for you: come quickly to us,
   gather to battle. God alone knows
   who shall carry the wielding of this waste ground.'

The war-wolves waded across, mourned not for the water,
the Viking warrior-band; came west over Pant,
bearing shield-boards over sheer water
and up onto land, lindenwood braced.

Against their wrath there stood in readiness
Bryhtnoth amid his band. He bade them work

the war-hedge with their targes, and the troop to stand
fast against foe. Then neared the fight,
the glory-trial. The time grew on
when there the fated men must fall;
the war-cry was raised up. Ravens wound higher,
the eagle, carrion-eager; on earth – the cry!

Out flashed file-hard point from fist,
sharp-ground spears sprang forth,
bows were busy, bucklers flinched,
it was a bitter battle-clash. On both halves
brave men fell, boys lay still.

It was then that Wulfmaer was wounded, war-rest chose,
Bryhtnoth's kinsman; he was beaten down,
his sister's son, under the swords' flailing.
But straight wreaking requital on the Vikings,
Edward (as I heard) so struck one man
– the sword-arm stiff, not stinting the blow –
that the fated warrior fell at his feet:
deed for which Bryhtnoth, when a breathing space came,
spoke his thanks to his bower-thane.

So they stood fast, those stout-hearted
warriors at the war-play, watching fiercely
who there with spear might first dispatch
a doomed man's life. The dying fell to earth;
others stood steadfast. Bryhtnoth stirred them,
bade every man there turn mood to deeds
who would that day's doom wrest from out the Danish ranks.

Bryhtnoth war-hard braced shield-board,
shook out his sword, strode firmly
toward his enemy, earl to churl,
in either's heart harm to the other.

The sea-man sped his southern spear
so that it wounded the warriors' lord
who with his shield checked, so that the shaft burst,

shivered the spear-head; it sprang away.
Stung then to anger he stabbed with ash-point
the proud sea-warrior that wrought him his wound,
old in war-skills let the weapon drive
through the man's throat, his thrust steered
so as to reach right to the reaver's life-breath.
And afresh he struck him, stabbed so swiftly
that the ring-braid burst apart; breast pierced
through the locked hauberk, in his heart stood
the embittered ash-point. The Earl was the blither,
his brave mood laughed, loud thanks he made
for the day's work the Lord had dealt him.

Flashed a dart from Danish hand,
fist-driven, and flew too truly,
bit the Earl, Aethelred's thane.
There stood at his side a stripling warrior,
young Wulfmaer, Wulfstan's son,
fresh to the field. In a flash he
plucked from its place the blood-black point,
flung back the filed spear; again it flew.
Home sank the steel, stretched on the plain
him who so late had pierced the Prince so grievously.

A mailed man then moved toward the Earl
thinking to strip him of his steel harness,
war-dress, armbands and ornate sword.
Bryhtnoth broke out brand from sheath,
broad, bright-bladed, and on the breastplate struck,
but one of the spoilers cut short the blow,
his swing unstringing the Earl's sword-arm.

He yielded to the ground the yellow-hilted sword,
strengthless to hold the hard blade longer up
or wield weapon. One word more,
the hoar-headed warrior, heartening his men:
he bade them go forward, good companions.
Fast on his feet he might not further stand;

he looked to heaven. . . .

'I give Thee thanks, Lord God of hosts,
for I have known in this world a wealth of gladness,
but now, mild Maker, I have most need
that Thou grant my ghost grace for this journey
so that my soul may unscathed cross
into Thy keeping, King of angels,
pass through in peace: my prayer is this,
that the hates of hell may not harm her.'

Then they hewed him down, the heathen churls,
and with him those warriors, Wulfmaer and Aelfnoth,
who had stood at his side: stretched on the field,
the two followers fellowed in death.

Then did the lack-willed leave the battlefield;
Odda's kin came first away:
Godric turned, betrayed the lord
who had made him a gift of many good horses.
He leapt onto the harness that had been Bryhtnoth's,
unrightfully rode in his place,
and with him his brothers both ran,
Godwine and Godwiy, who had no gust for fighting;
they wheeled from the war to the wood's fastness,
sought shelter and saved their lives;
and more went with them than were at all meet
had they called to mind the many heart-claims
Bryhtnoth had wrought them, worthying them.

This Offa had told him on an earlier day
at the council-place when he had called a meeting,
that many gathered there who were making brave speeches
would not hold in the hour of need.
And now the folk's father had fallen lifeless,
Aethelred's Earl. All the hearthsharers
might see their lord lying dead.

Proudly the thanes pressed forward,

uncowed the warriors crowded eager
for one of two things: each man wanted
either to requite that death or to quit life.
Aelfric's son sped them on,
a warrior young in winters; his words rang
keen in the air. Aelfwine called out:

'Remember the speeches spoken over mead,
battle-vows on the bench, the boasts we vaunted,
heroes in hall, against the harsh war-trial!
Now shall be proven the prowess of the man.

I would that you all hear my high descendance:
know that in Mercia I am of mighty kin,
that my grandfather was the great Ealhelm,
wise Earl, world-blessed man.
Shall the princes of that people reproach Aelfwine
that he broke from the banded bulwark of the Angles
to seek his own land, with his lord lying
felled on the field? Fiercest of griefs!
Beside that he was my lord he was allied to me in blood.'

Then he advanced on the Vikings intent on vengeance.
Straight his spearpoint sprang at a man
among the press of pirates, pitched him to the ground,
killed outright. Then he called to his companions
friends and fellow-thanes to come forth to battle.

Offa spoke, shook his ash-spear:

'In right good time dost thou recall us to
our allegiance, Aelfwine. Now that the Earl who led us
lies on the earth, we all need
each and every thane to urge forth the other
warriors to the war while weapon lives
quick in a hand, hardened blade,
spear or good sword. Godric the coward,
the coward son of Odda, has undone us all:
too many in our ranks, when he rode away

on Bryhtnoth's big horse, believed it was the Earl,
and we are scattered over the field. The folk is split,
shield-wall shattered. Shame on that defection
that has betrayed into retreat the better half of the army!'
Linden-board high-lifted, Leofsunu stood;
from the shadow of his shield shouted out this answer:

'I swear that from this spot not one foot's space
of ground shall I give up. I shall go onwards,
in the fight avenge my friend and lord.
My deeds shall give no warrant for words of blame
to steadfast men on Stour, now he is stretched
                                                           lifeless,
– that I left the battlefield a lordless man,
turned for home. The irons shall take me,
point or edge.'
                        Angrily he strode forth
and fought very fiercely; flight was beneath him.

Dart brandished, Dunnere spoke,
bidding his brothers avenge Bryhtnoth.
The humble churl called out over all:

'A man cannot linger when his lord lies
unavenged among Vikings, cannot value breath.'

So the household companions, careless of life,
bore spears to battle and set to bitter fighting:
they went out into the press, praying God
that among their enemies they might so acquit themselves
as to redress the death of their dear lord.

The hostage lent them help willingly;
he was a Northumbrian of a hard-fighting clan,
the son of Edgeleave, Ashferth his name;
wavered not at the war-play, but, while he might,
shot steadily from his sheaf of arrows,
striking a shield there, or shearing into a man,
and every once in a while wounding wryly.

At that time Long Edward still led the attack,
breathing his readiness, rolling out boasts
that nothing would budge him now that the best man lay,
nothing force him to flee one foot of ground.
He broke the board-wall, burst in among them,
wrought on the sea-wreckers a revenge worthy
his goldgiving lord before the ground claimed him.

So did the noble Aetheric, another of our company,
he too fought fixedly, furious to get on,
Sibyrht's brother; and so did many another,
cleaving in halves the hollow shields.
Board's border burst asunder,
corselet sang its chilling song.
How they beat off the blows!
                          At the battle's turn
Off sent a seafarer stumbling to the ground;
but crippling strokes crashed down
and Gadd's kinsman was grounded also.

Yet Offa had made good his given word,
the oath undertaken to his open-handed lord,
that either they should both ride back to the burg's stockade,
come home whole, or harry the Danes
till life leaked from them and left them on the field.
Thane-like he lay at his lord's hand.

Then was a splintering of shields, the sea-wolves coming on
in war-whetted anger. Again the spears
burst breast-lock, breached life-wall
of Wierd-singled men. Wistan went forth,
that Wurstan fathered, fought with the warriors
where they thronged thickest. Three he slew
before the breath was out of Offa's body.

It was a stark encounter, but they stood their ground –
the warriors in that fight, fought till wounds
dragged them down. The dead fell.
All the while Eadwold and Oswold his brother

cried on their kinsmen, encouraging them
to stand up under the stress, strike out the hour,
weaving unwavering the web of steel.
Then Bryhtwold spoke, shook ash-spear,
raised shield-board. In the bravest words
this hoar companion handed on the charge:

'Courage shall grow keener, clearer the will,
the heart fiercer, as our force faileth.
Here our lord lies levelled in the dust,
the man all marred: he shall mourn to the end
who thinks to wend off from this war-play now.
Though I am white with winters I will not away,
for I think to lodge me alongside my dear one,
lay me down by my lord's right hand.'

Godric likewise gave them all heart,
Aethelgar's son, sending spears,
death-darts, driving on the Danish ranks;
likewise he forged foremost among them,
scattering blows, bowing at last.

That was not the Godric who galloped away. . . .

NOTES

———— z ————

THOUGH I have consulted all the editions usually available, I have relied on three books more than any others in making these translations. The standard edition of Old English texts is *The Anglo-Saxon Poetic Records*, by G. P. Krapp and E. V. K. Dobbie, published in six volumes by the Columbia University Press (Routledge and Kegan Paul in England). Volume III, *The Exeter Book*, has been particularly useful to me, and I have followed the readings of Krapp and Dobbie except where I have noted to the contrary. There is a very convenient 'bilingual' edition of *The Exeter Book* in the Early English Text Society series, and I have frequently used W. S. Mackie's edition of the second part of the Book. The third book to which I have constantly had recourse is Bosworth and Toller's *An Anglo-Saxon Dictionary* (Oxford), still, unfortunately, the only Anglo-Saxon English dictionary which attempts completeness, and still in two unwieldy volumes. For individual poems I have often used separate editions, acknowledged below. Most of these originally appeared in Methuen's Old English Library, then Manchester University Press and now published by Exeter University as medieval English texts.

All line references are to the Anglo-Saxon text.

THE RUIN (p. 1)

There are several difficult passages, and my attempts to translate the defective lines, wherever it was feasible, should not be taken as more than guesses.

l. 4. I read *hrim geat berofen, hrim on lime*, accepting the repetition of *hrim*, but not of *torras* from line 3.

l. 12. I read *wonað giet se wealstan wæpnum geheawen* with Mackie.

l. 18. *hygerof* seems to imply some such interpretation of the first part of the line.

l. 22. *horngestreon* — with a wealth of gables. The hall-gables were often made to appear more fearsome by means of horn-ornaments. See the description of Heorot in *Beowulf*.

l. 26. Mackie seems to suggest that *secgrof* may be the equivalent of Latin *robur*.

l. 31. I follow Mackie's reading.

DEOR *and* WIDSITH

Prefatory Note

1. R. W. Chambers, *Widsith*, p. 181.

2. Chambers, p. 6.

3. That of Wade, l. 22. See note below.

4. 'In the catalogue of kings Gifica rules the Burgundians, Meaca the Myrgings, Sceafa the Lombards. In the Ealhhild-Eormanric portion Guthere rules the Burgundians, Eadgils the Myrgings, Eadwine and Aelfwine the Lombards.' Chambers, p. 134.

Deor (p. 14)

I have used Dobbie's notes and relied on his text throughout. Kemp Malone's edition of the poem in Methuen's Old English Library (1933) is very convenient and informative.

l. 1. *Welund.* In the *Völundarkviða*, Volundr is captured by Nithhad and hamstrung so that he should not escape. However, he does escape (which is the point of the allusion), killing Nithhad's two sons and raping his daughter into the bargain. The daughter, Beadohild, bears the hero Widia; which, though left unsaid, is the silver lining of the next strophe.

Wrenn writes that the cult of Wayland, whose name means Artificer, originates in the belief that iron swords possessed magic powers; so it must have seemed to the Germanic tribes still using bronze swords when they came up against Celts in the sixth century before Christ. Wayland is thus the counterpart of the Roman Vulcan. That he was well known in England is attested by the early Northumbrian Franks Casket, a whalebone and tin box now in the British Museum; one face (see cover) shows Wayland drinking out of the skull of one of Nithhad's sons. And the story goes, that if a man tethers his horses at Wayland's Smithy (a group of stones on the Berkshire Downs), and leaves payment there, he will find the horse shod on his return.

be wurman: despite many efforts at emendation this phrase remains unintelligible, and I have omitted it from my translation. Malone is the only editor to have tried to make sense of the text as it stands; he suggests that *wurman* refers to the serpentine inlay upon the sword with which Wayland was maimed.

l. 6. *seonobende:* sinew-bonds, bonds caused by cutting the sinews.

l. 14. I read *mæð Hild* with Grein, and follow Mackie's interpretation. Who Hild (or, for that matter, Maethhild, as she becomes in some editions) was, is quite unknown, as is Geat (or *the* Geat), her lover.

l. 18. This Theodric is the Ostrogoth, Dietrich von Bern, the greatest hero of medieval German poetry. The misfortune lies, as Miss Ashdown suggests, in the fact that he held the Maering city (Verona) for thirty years only, and held it no longer – being exiled by Eormanric; this involves a perfective sense for *ahte*. Deor cheers himself with the reflection that exile can befall the greatest. This seems the best of the many constructions which have been put on this exceptionally cryptic reference.

In his edition of *Widsith* (Cambridge, 1912) Chambers discusses very fully the historical and ethnographical features of the poem. My prefatory note and the facts contained in these notes and in the Glossary of Proper Names owe a great debt to him. Dobbie's notes are also useful, and I have followed his text.

Widsith (p. 16)

l. 2. I read *se þe monna mæst mægþa ofer eorþan* with Grein and most editors.

l. 4. I translate with Mackie, who accepts Thorpe's emendation to *him*, though Dobbie implies, perhaps accidentally, that he does not. For the Myrgings, see the Glossary of Proper Names.

l. 5. *Ealhhild.* This daughter of Eadwine (l. 74) is apparently the sister of Alboin the Lombard (l. 99), and her marriage to Eormanric is meant to be a bond between Lombards and Goths. The Lombards lived on the lower Elbe, immediately next to the Myrgings and the Angles, before moving south into Italy. It is possible that she is to be identified with the Sunilda of the Latin historian Jordanes, a woman whom Eormanric orders to be torn in half by horses as a punishment for the revolt of her husband. See Chambers, pp. 15 ff.

l. 8. *eastan of Ongle:* 'from the East, from Angel.'

l. 9. *wraþes wærlogan.* Eormanric is a tyrant in *Deor* and in most later tradition; he is presented in *Widsith* as extraordinarily generous.

Greatness and generosity were always associated. The reputation for cruelty may come, Chambers suggests, from the sentence of death passed on Sunilda (see above).

ll. 21-2. The story of Hagen and Heoden is one of the most popular of Germanic tales. Chambers quotes the four complete versions of it extant, and shows that the mention of Wade in the next line is not accidental. Wade was a sea-giant, a supernatural not a historic character, though he has here become the king of the Halsings. The core of the story is that Heoden loves Hild, the daughter of King Hagen, and sends Heorrenda, his minstrel, to woo for him. Heorrenda's magic song persuades the girl to escape, and she and Heorrenda flee to Heoden's court in Wade's magic boat. Hagen pursues his daughter, and he and his men fight Heoden and his followers (on the island of Hoy, in the Orkneys, according to Snorri Sturluson). Hagen is killed. But Snorri's account ends differently:

> Then they began the battle, which is called *Hjathningavig*; and they fought all the day, and in the evening the kings went to their ships. But Hild went by night to the corpses, and awoke the dead by magic. And the next day the kings went to the battlefield and fought, and so did all those who fell the day before.
>
> In such wise the battle continued, day after day; so that all those who fell, and all the weapons and shields which lay on the battlefield, were turned into stone. And when it dawned, all the dead men stood up and fought, and all the weapons were sound: and it is told in songs that the Hjathningar shall so abide till Doomsday . . .

Heorrenda occurs in *Deor* as the poet who replaces Deor at the court of the Heodenings. Wade's boat is mentioned in *The Merchant's Tale* and also in *Troilus*, when Pandare 'tolde tale of Wade' to Criseyde. Chambers has a fascinating section on Wade, but cannot ultimately add much to Speght's celebrated note in his edition of Chaucer (1598): 'Concerning Wade and his bote called Guingelot, as also his strange exploits in the same, because the matter is long and fabulous, I passe it over.'

ll. 25-8. All the tribes mentioned here were neighbours of the Angles in Denmark.

l. 35. *Offa weold Ongle*. This praise of Offa the Angle, which is inappropriate in the mouth of a Myrging *scop*, is one of the main reasons for thinking that *Widsith* was composed or revised in the reign of Offa of Mercia, his descendant in the twelfth generation if we are to believe the genealogies. Offa here is the founder of Angel. The story referred to is told, with variations, by

two Danish historians at the end of the twelfth century, Sweyn
Aageson and Saxo Grammaticus. In essence, it is the story of
Offa's duel on the island of Fifeldor at the mouth of the Eider
against two Myrgings – the prince of the Swaefe, and a chosen
champion. The 'single sword' is an important part of this dramatic
tale, which is summarized in Chambers' Introduction.

l. 36. It is indicative of the extent of our ignorance that the name of
Alewih, 'the boldest of all those (the foregoing) men', is otherwise
completely unknown.

ll. 45 ff. These five lines refer to the famous alliance between two
members of the house of Scyld, the Scylding family which ruled
the Danes. Hrothgar is the most important character in *Beowulf*
apart from the hero himself; the action of the first part of the
poem takes place at Heorot, Hrothgar's hall. Hrothwulf is the son
of Halga, Hrothgar's younger brother. Hrothgar favoured his
famous nephew greatly; between them they overcame (as is related
here) the Heathobards under their chief, Ingeld.

From *Beowulf* it seems that Hrothgar married his daughter
Freawaru to the young leader of the Heathobards, Ingeld, in hope
of healing an ancient feud between Danes and Heathobards in
which Froda, Ingeld's father, had lost his life. At his return home,
one of Ingeld's own retainers kills one of Freawaru's Danish
followers; and the feud is resurrected again. In subsequent fighting
at Heorot Ingeld and his followers are slain.

This much is stated in these five lines. But a further tragic event
in the history of the Scylding house is clearly foreshadowed in
lengest; it is said that the kinsmen kept faith together 'for a very
long time' after this famous victory. This is seemingly a way of
implying that the pact was eventually broken; Hrothwulf repays
Hrothgar's generosity in fostering and protecting him, even to the
point where he, the nephew, had eclipsed Hrothgar's own two
sons, by murdering the sons and usurping the Danish throne after
the death of their father.

This truly laconic sentence, resuming the whole history of one
generation of the Scylding house, is paralleled by the equally
tight-lipped stanzas of *Deor*. The fortunes of the house of Scyld
must have been as well-known on both sides of the North Sea as
were those of the house of Atreus throughout the Aegean centuries
before. They are alluded to in the same grim way as were the
complicated and bloody stories of the inhabitants of the palace of
Mycenae. *Beowulf* is irritatingly cryptic about those tales of the
conflict of personal and social loyalty which loom in the wings of

the monster-slaying story which is its main theme. But that the characters of this particular episode were well-known is testified by their occurrence all over the Viking countries in later tradition (e.g. in *Hrolfssaga Kraki* and in Saxo Grammaticus). Ingeld was popular enough in story for Alcuin, writing in 797 to the monks of Lindisfarne, to conclude his epistle (which recommends them to listen to the Scriptures and the doctrine of the Fathers of the Church rather than to the harp and to heathen songs) by the rhetorical question: '*Quid enim Hinieldus cum Christo?*'

l. 57. *Hreð-Gotum*: another name for the Goths. Huns and Goths were traditionally enemies.

l. 63. The three tribes mentioned in this line probably lived in modern Norway.

ll. 65–7. Guthere (see Glossary of Proper Names) later became identified with the King of the Volsungs; in the *Nibelungenlied*, in *Thrithreks Saga* and in the *Volsunga Saga*, Gunter and Hagen betray Siegfried the Volsung and rob him of his bride, his gold, and his life. See Chambers, pp. 58 ff.

ll. 75–87. The interpolated catalogue.

l. 83. Perhaps an attempt to reconcile passages like 38–44, where the poet is apparently opposed to the Myrgings, with 93–6 (Chambers' suggestion).

l. 87. Probably (see Chambers) three tribes inhabiting the Baltic provinces of Russia.

ll. 88–9. Or 'all of which time the Gothic King was kind towards me.'

l. 91. Chambers calculates that the ring may have weighed as much as ten ounces of refined gold; it was, of course, an arm-ring, not a finger-ring.

l. 93. Chambers shows that Eadgils was probably a historical king of the Myrgings, and that it was his killing of an Anglian chief which started the feud terminated by Offa at Fifeldor (see note to l.35 above, and Chambers, pp. 92–4).

l. 104. 'our lord in war': Eadgils.

ll. 112 ff. Hethca and Beadeca do not belong among the Gothic heroes. The Herelings are Emerca and Fridla, Eormanric's nephews, put to death by his order. East-Gota is the founder of the Ostrogothic fortunes. Seafola (Sabene) is one of Theodric's most faithful retainers. Secca and Heathoric are unidentified. Sifeca persuaded Eormanric to murder the Herelings. Theodric, the greatest of the Ostrogoths, was exiled (in legend) from Verona by Eormanric.

The names Eadwine, Elsa, Aegelmund, Hungar and With-Myrgingas are probably interpolated; two of them are Lombards, and none has any relevance to the wars of the Goths and Huns. Hlithe and Incgentheow were half-brothers who fought on opposite sides in these wars. Wulfhere and Wormhere are unknown, but are plausible Gothic names.

Finally we come to the legendary battle between the Goths and the Huns (under Attila) *ymb Wistlawudu*. The Goths had left the Vistula by the end of the second century, and at that time Attila was unborn and the Huns unheard of. The long struggle between the peoples took place on the plains north of the Black Sea in the fourth century. But however unhistoric the chronology and geography of this passage, the antiquity of the saga-tradition it preserves can be felt even across the intervening centuries. The wood – Mirkwood, as it is called in Icelandic legend – *was* the ancient hearthland of the Goths. It was natural that in such a battle all the famous names of Gothic story should be ranged with Eormanric, in whose reign the threat of the Huns was first felt, and that the Huns should be led by their most feared leader, Attila.

The names in l. 123 all belong to the Gothic cycle, though the last, Gislhere, was certainly a Burgundian. Freotheric may be Eormanric's son. Only with Wudga (Widia) and Hama do we emerge into the comparative clarity of often-recorded names; see the Glossary of Proper Names.

BEOWULF *and* THE FIGHT AT FINNSBURG

I have relied on C. L. Wrenn's edition of *Beowulf* (3rd edition, rev. Bolton, London 1973); but for *Finnsburg* I have also used F. Klaeber's *Beowulf and the Fight at Finnsburg* (3rd edition, Boston and London, 1951) and *The Anglo-Saxon Poetic Records*, vol. VI.

Prefatory Note

1. Wrenn suggests that Scyld means 'protector', Shefing 'with a sheaf' – i.e. bringing prosperity. The Danish ruling house were called Scyldingas – i.e. 'the men of the shield'; but to make their origin more specific, the founder is given the eponymous name of Scyld, and -*ingas* becomes a patronymic. His advent is rather like that of Moses in the bulrushes – and of other epiphanies.

2. No body was found in the ship, and Mr Bruce-Mitford, in a

note of introduction to the fifth impression of *The British Museum Provisional Guide to the Sutton Hoo Ship Burial*, wrote: 'it now seems reasonable to think that the ship-burial, considered as a cenotaph (one could not take this view if it had contained a body) may be a public monument in a traditional manner to Aethelhere's Christian predecessor and brother, Anna (d. 654), whose body we have reason to believe was buried in consecrated ground at Blythburgh, not far from Sutton Hoo. A grave like that at Sutton Hoo, very richly furnished and in a pagan burial-place, could, in an East Anglian royal context after 650, only be a pagan burial. Such a furnished mound, however, *without a body*, might still at that late date and in that context, be possible in a half-Christian kingdom as a public memorial to an important king who had himself given up reliance on pagan customs in favour of Christian burial.' The publication of Bruce-Mitford's monograph on Sutton Hoo was completed in 1983.

The last lines of *The Seafarer* specifically deny the utility of burying one's brother with the golden things one would have him take. See ll. 97–102 n.

3. As does *Dr Zhivago*.
4. Roskilde was the home of the Danish Kings in the Middle Ages.
5. See W. P. Ker, *Epic and Romance*, p. 10.
6. Either of whom may be identified with Hunlafing.
7. In Chapter 2 of *The Beginnings of English Society*.
8. Quite possibly the Hengest of history, who invaded Kent with Horsa ('horse'); Hengest, oddly enough, means 'stallion'.

Beowulf: lines 26–52 (p. 26)

l. 30. *wordum*: There seems to be no reason why this should not mean 'by his words', though Wrenn does not mention the possibility.
l. 37. *of feor-wegum*: from far countries. Nearly all the silver in the Sutton Hoo treasure comes from the Mediterranean.
l. 43. This deliberate understatement is very typical of Old English heroic verse.
l. 47. *segen: signum*. One of the dozen Latin-derived words in *Beowulf*.

Beowulf: lines 194–257 (p. 27)

l. 194. 'one of Hygelac's followers': Beowulf. Hygelac is, in fact, Beowulf's uncle.

l. 199. 'the warrior king': Hrothgar.

l. 203. 'hardly or not at all': typical litotes. The elders encouraged Beowulf in his idea.

l.204. 'watched omens': Wrenn cites *Germania*, 10: *Auspicia sortesque ut qui maxime observant.*

l. 209. *lagu-cræftig mon*: Beowulf, not a pilot. Wrenn's note.

l. 225. 'Weather-Geats': the Geats are called *Wederas* by virtue of their seafaring habits, as Wrenn suggests.

l. 247. *maga gemedu*: 'the consent of the kinsmen'. Hrothgar and Hrothwulf are thought of as ruling the land jointly.

Beowulf: lines 837–75 (p. 29)

l. 837. *mine gefræge:* 'as I have heard tell'; the traditional formula.

l. 840. 'the wonder': Grendel's arm, which Beowulf has torn off and placed on one of the gables of Heorot.

l. 842. 'not . . . one man sorry'; litotes again.

l. 850. *deog:* 'died', following Wrenn.

l. 871. *soðe gebunden:* 'truly bound together' – i.e. by alliteration. Or possibly, 'adorned with truth', as Wrenn suggests. His note is interesting.

l. 874. *wordum wrixlan:* 'rang word-changes'. Wrenn: '. . . looks so very much like a direct allusion to the poetic technique of "variation" – so marked a stylistic feature of Old English verse – that the balance seems to swing in favour of taking *soðe gebunden* as referring to alliteration. Editors have compared *Sir Gawain and the Green Knight* 35 – "with lel letteres loken".'

l. 875. *Sigemunde:* The *scop* is made to compare Beowulf with the greatest of all the dragon-slayers of Germanic tradition, Sigemund in the English tradition, Siguthur in the Old Icelandic Eddas and in the Volsung Sagas, Siegfried in the *Nibelungenlied*. Sigemund slays the treasure-guarding dragon: but the hoard has a death-curse upon it. Beowulf's own end is foreshadowed. See Wrenn's Introduction for further discussion.

Beowulf: lines 2231–66 (p. 30)

l. 2241. The barrow is situated on a headland, like the barrow in which the ashes of Beowulf himself are to be buried.

The Fight at Finnsburg (p. 33)

l. 1. A reconstruction. I read *Hnæf*, not *næfre*.

l. 18. *styrode*; I read *styrde* with Chambers.

l. 28. I read *wealle*, not *healle*.

l. 29. *celæs borth*; Hickes' text is obviously corrupt. *cellod bord* is usually supplied from *Maldon*, 283, and that is what I have tried to translate.

l. 34. I have accepted Holthausen's emendation to *hwearf blacra hræs*.

l. 43. It is not clear whether the warrior who retires is a Frisian or a Dane, though *folces hyrde* indicates Finn rather than Hengest, who was only a deputy for Hnaef. Perhaps this is a preliminary to Finn's decision to call a truce.

WALDERE

I have relied largely on the text of F. Norman's edition in the Methuen Old English Library, but have also consulted Van Kirk Dobbie in vol. VI of *The Anglo-Saxon Poetic Records*. Norman's edition is to be recommended, and I owe most of my facts to him.

Prefatory Note

1. The Hagen of the Nibelungen; always teamed up with Gunther in Northern tradition. In *Waldere* Gunther and Hagen are Burgundians, not Franks as they are in *Waltharius*.

2. The poet, as Norman suggests, is trying to forestall the objections of his audience, who must have known that the sword belonged by right to Widia.

3. Norman, pp. 15–18. It certainly seems odd that Waldere should resume his speech in this way. But if *eac* means 'also', as Klaeber says, then the speaker of these first ten lines is almost certainly the owner of Mimming.

4. Ker's discussion of *Waldere* (*Epic and Romance*, pp. 84–8) is worth reading in this connection.

Waldere (p. 38)

1, l. 1. *Hildeguth*. This would be the Old English form of Hiltgunt; though the name does not occur in the Anglo-Saxon fragments, the inference that it is Hildeguth who delivers this speech is straightforward, and I have made it explicit.

I, l. 5. *secg æfter oðrum.* referring to the twelve knights of *Waltharius*; in which case, Waldere has been using Mimming already, and is not keeping it in reserve (II, 3).

I, l. 12. *wordum cide*: cf. *wordum ætwitan* in *Maldon*, 250, where the thought is much the same.

I, l. 15. *weal*: 'baulk', the natural protection afforded by the defile.

I, l. 24. *ði mece*: 'thy sword'. Ambiguous; but whichever sword Waldere is using first, it breaks in the fight against Gunther, according to *Waltharius*.

I, l. 31. *swefan*: 'sleep'. The habit of sarcastic euphemism is strong in Old English heroic verse.

II, l. 3. *stanfate*. The context seems to indicate that this means 'sheath', and not the 'silver chests', which is the meaning usually given to 'syncfatum' (I, 28).

II, l. 4–12. *it* could refer to the sword in the sheath just mentioned, or, equally well, to the other sword. Norman shows that Mimming was probably the reward which Theodoric the Ostrogoth sent to Widia in gratitude for his rescue from the Giants. This rescue is referred to in several Middle High German sources cited by Norman. Widia was Wayland's son (and Nithhad's grandson), and it is therefore appropriate that he should be the owner of his father's handiwork. Mimming is here given to Waldere by the attraction that exists between famous swords and famous heroes.

THE WANDERER *and* THE SEAFARER

For *The Wanderer* I have used Dobbie's text, except where noted. *The Seafarer* is edited separately in Methuen's Old English Library by I. L. Gordon, on whose text I have relied. Sweet's *Reader* contains both poems, Mackie *The Seafarer* only. Both are well translated by N. Kershaw in *Anglo-Saxon and Norse Poems* (Cambridge, 1922).

Prefatory Note

1. *The Beginnings of English Society*, pp. 36–7.
2. *Word-Hoard*, pp. 67–8. Alfred's authorship is doubtful.
3. Dobbie agrees with Miss Kershaw in placing the end of the first speech at line 29a of *The Wanderer*, although in his text the final quotation marks have by some accident been omitted. But whether the speech ends here or at line 63, which is where I have put it,

following Sweet, makes very little difference to the basic structure of the poem.

4. I have in the second edition restored the devout endings of *The Seafarer* and *The Dream of the Rood* in prose renderings. Though conscious of the Christian contribution to Old English, and of the disadvantages of editorial analysis, I still regard these endings as later expansions, certainly in the case of the latter poem.

5. Pound's 'Angles' for 'angels' is as notorious as Gregory the Great's original pun. Indeed, his suppression of Christian references is so complete that his *Seafarer* can be searched in vain for any evidence that the conversion of England ever took place. This suppression was quite conscious. See the discussion in my *Poetic Achievement of Ezra Pound*, pp. 66–79.

The Wanderer (p. 48)

l. 1. *gebideð* can mean either 'expects', 'waits for' or 'experiences'. Most who give *The Wanderer* a Christian interpretation, adopt this latter meaning – i.e. that the *anhaga* actually experiences the Lord's mercy in the end. But, though this perfective sense is certainly well attested, the overall pattern of the poem, and even of the prologue itself, has seemed to me to argue against it.

l. 6. *eardstapa*: see Prefatory Note.

l. 13. 'A woman may decently express her grief in public; a man should nurse his in his heart.' Tacitus, *Germania*, 27.

l. 27. I accept Klaeber's insertion of *min* before *mine wisse*.

ll. 42–3. This probably refers to some ritual of fealty.

l. 53. *eft* makes much better sense than *oft*.

l. 62. *middangeard*: Professor Coghill suggested to me that the always latent parallel between *middangeard* and the Scandinavian *Midgarth* (the abode of men, as opposed to *Asgarth*, the home of the gods) should be borne in mind here.

ll. 70–2. It was customary to boast at the ale-drinking of the feats one would perform in battle; see *Maldon*, 212, where the noble Aelfwine reminds his companions of 'the battle-vows on the bench'. Mrs Ellis Davidson, in her chapter on the Gods of Battle, remarks that in Valhalla, 'men were said to divide their time between battle and drinking. These were two means by which they could while on earth achieve forgetfulness of self, and it is therefore fitting that they should be the only occupations in Odin's hall.' H. R. Ellis Davidson, *Gods and Myths of Northern Europe*, p. 70.

l. 81. *summe fugel opbær*: literally 'one a bird bore off'. Dobbie in his note favours Thorpe's figurative interpretation of the bird as a ship; this would be a reference then to a ship-burial. It is true that a ship is often spoken of as being *fugle gelicost* – most like a bird – as in *Beowulf* l. 218; but the raven and the wolf, animals sacred to Odin, are always on the scene of any battle. And there seems no need why the wolf should be a metaphor for exile, as Dobbie suggests.

l. 87. 'giant-works'. See the prefatory note to *The Ruin*.

The Seafarer (p. 52)

l. 1. Compare the opening of *The Wife's Complaint*.

l. 16. The second half of this line is presumed to have been omitted by accident.

ll. 19–24. I. L. Gordon ornithologises. Concurring with Mrs Goldsmith that 'we cannot identify all the species exactly, since from the evidence of glosses it appears that the Anglo-Saxons did not make the clear distinctions between the species that are made now', she remarks on *huilpan* (l. 21): 'Miss Daunt (MLR xiii. 478) and Miss Kershaw would identify the bird as the bar-tailed godwit or "yarwhelp". But both the modern English and Scottish dialect *whaup* and the cognate Low German forms, such as Dutch *wulp*, Frisian *wilp*, are used of the curlew (see *NED* s. whaup) and this is pretty clearly the generic sense, the godwit being called "yarwhelp" because it resembles the curlew. Many curlews are summer visitors only, but there are always some that remain round our coast in winter.'

ll. 24–5. My translation condenses the Anglo-Saxon; the repetition of *isigfeðera* and *urigfeðera*, and the lack of alliteration in line 25 make it virtually certain that the text is corrupt.

l. 26. Grein's *frefran*, comfort, for *feran* is convincing.

l. 33. *corna caldast*: 'coldest of grains'. My translation conserves the visual side of the image. I. L. Gordon shows that there is reason to think that this was a magical formula, the hailstones being thought of as seeds of winter; she cites the Old Norwegian Rune Song: *Hagall er kaldastr korna*, and the Old English Runic Poem: *Hægl byþ hwitust corna*. See also the Appendix A on the Runes.

l. 40. *ne his gifena þæs god*; 'nor so well endowed'.

l. 53. The cuckoo is thought of as bringing sorrow both here and in *The Husband's Message*, whereas everywhere else in Germanic literature the cuckoo is the harbinger of spring (as well as of cuckoldry). The cuckoo is a bird of lament in Welsh poetry, and for the undoubted Welsh influence on the elegies Mrs Gordon's introduction (pp. 15–18) should be read.

ll. 64–6. If it were not for these lines one could disregard the 'Christianizing' interpretation of this poem put forward by G. V. Smithers, and accepted by many scholars.

l. 81. My translation is a variation on Pound's 'and all arrogance of earthen riches', which cannot be bettered, although *rices* does not mean 'riches'.

ll. 97–102. I read *wille* with Dobbie (and with the MS), though Mrs Gordon's note is interesting: 'Miss Kershaw refers to *Ynglinga saga*, chap. 8, where it is stated that according to Odin's promise everyone shall bring to Valhalla such treasure as was placed on his funeral pyre and also what he had himself hidden in the ground during his lifetime.'

THE WIFE'S COMPLAINT, THE HUSBAND'S MESSAGE, WULF AND EADWACER

I have relied upon Dobbie's introduction, text and notes, and have found Mackie's translations useful. Miss Kershaw's *Anglo-Saxon and Norse Poems* contains excellent translations.

The Wife's Complaint (p. 58)

l. 15. *herheard*: I have followed the majority of editors in taking this as *her heard*, but Grein suggested, very plausibly, that we should read *herh-eard*, meaning a dwelling in a (sacred) grove.

l. 24. There is an omission after *nu* in the text.

l. 42. I have taken these lines on the *smylere* as directed against the person responsible for the estrangement – the Iago of this affair. This seems simpler than Dobbie's interpretation, which is not fully clear to me.

The Husband's Message (p. 60)

ll. 1–7. Only a limited reconstruction is possible, but it is obvious that the staff is giving its personal history previous to this errand.

ll. 32–9. Translated along the lines suggested in Dobbie's notes. It is fair to guess that the word omitted before 'of men' was *holdra*; the

implication being that the husband had enough loyal followers to
tell his wife to come.

l. 48. I have taken *ofer* as meaning 'over and above', and hope to
have implied this in the syntax. A new sentence seems to begin
with *gecyre*.

l. 50. See Appendix A on Runes for a proposed solution.

Wulf and Eadwacer (p. 62)

Dobbie says that there are some similarities between the apparent
situation in this poem and that in the Wolfdietrich B story; but no
conclusive identification has been suggested.

l. 9. *wenum dogode*: meaning either 'suffered from hopes of' or 'was
thinking of' (if *hogode* is accepted). The metre is odd, and I have
taken the simpler meaning.

l. 16. *earne*: cowardly, or *eargne*: miserable. Both, I hope, are implied
in 'whelp'.

GNOMIC VERSES (p. 63)

I have again relied on Dobbie for text and notes, and found Mackie's
translations of use. Miss B. C. Williams's *Gnomic Poetry in Anglo-
Saxon* (Columbia University Press, 1914) is valuable.

Prefatory Note

1. Some charms are translated in S. A. J. Bradley's *Anglo-Saxon Poetry*
(Everyman, 1982); see also Mrs Ellis Davidson's *Gods and Myths of
Northern Europe*.

2. *Gnomic Poetry in Anglo-Saxon*, pp. 92 ff.

3. 'The dowry is brought by husband to wife, not by wife to husband.
Parents and kinsmen attend and approve of the gifts, gifts not chosen
to please a woman's whim or gaily deck a young bride, but oxen,
horse with reins, shield, spear and sword. For such gifts a man gets
his wife, and she in her turn brings some present of arms to her
husband. In this interchange of gifts they recognize the supreme
bond, the holy mysteries, the presiding deities of marriage.' Tacitus,
Germania, 18.

l. 78. *deop deada wæg*: this could also mean 'the deep way of the
dead'; in any case it is parallel with *sund unstille*.

l. 95. The Frisians are always spoken of as seafarers.

RIDDLES (p. 67)

Dobbie's introduction, text and notes have again been of the greatest use, though it is pleasant to read the riddles in Mackie's bilingual versions. I have adopted the numbering used by Mackie.

Prefatory Note

1. Chapter 2, verse 19. Douai version.

Riddle 12. Dobbie quotes the end of a riddle by Eusebius which makes it obvious that Riddle 12 is borrowed from Latin models, though the penultimate section is scarcely monastic.

ll. 4, 8. 'Welsh' in Anglo-Saxon meant simply 'foreigner'; the Romans are 'Rome-Welsh'. Tyroleans refer to Italians as Welsh. The walnut, coming from Italy, was called a 'welsh nut'. However, there is no reason to suppose that the Welsh serfs referred to here were not Celts.

Riddle 26. The solution is obvious. There are several Latin analogues to this riddle, and there is a riddle by Tatwine which apparently parallels the Christian development here, though no direct translation can be shown.

l. 8. I have adopted Dobbie's suggestion that Grein's insertion of *sprengde* before *speddropum* is not necessary, as one can take *geond* with *mec*.

l. 17. *nales dol wite*; Bosworth-Toller gives evidence that *dol* was used in the senses 'dull, foolish, erring, heretical'.

Riddle 27. For the reference to honey in line 5, compare Riddle 79.

Riddle 30. Wood is the solution given, but it has not quite the same applications as the Old English *beam*, which, as Blackburn pointed out, can mean 'tree', 'ship', 'log', 'harp', 'cup', 'cross'. I do not follow him in thinking that 'ship' is meant in l. 3a – a branch of a tree could be *fus forðweges* – or that a harp is referred to in l. 5, where 'cup' would be more natural. The last lines of this riddle contain the idea which is the heart of *The Dream of the Rood*.

Riddle 35. This is apparently a translation of Aldhelm's Riddle 33, *lorica*. There is also a Northumbrian version extant in the University Library at Leiden.

l. 9. *wyrda cræftum*: 'with skill given by the Wierds'. That the Loom of Fate is woven by three sisters is a world-wide idea. See N.

Kershaw's translation of the horrific *Darraðarljoð* in *Anglo-Saxon and Norse Poems*, and H. R. Ellis Davidson's *Gods and Myths of Northern Europe*, p. 64.

Riddle 38. Very similar to Riddle 12 and to various Latin riddles. I translate the last couplet with Mackie.

Riddle 42. The runes (see Appendix) spell out *hana* and *hæn* – cock and hen.

Riddle 57. The last half-line, *nemnað hy sylfe*, may mean 'they name themselves' – i.e. that the birds' names are formed from their characteristic call. Jackdaws and crows have been proposed.

Riddle 60. A variation upon *Arundo* (*Reed*) of Symphosius, itself a version of the story of Syrinx in Ovid's *Metamorphoses*. Compare *The Husband's Message*.

Riddle 68. The first two lines of this riddle and the third and last line are written out in *The Exeter Book* as two separate riddles, of which the first is probably incomplete. I have, for simplicity's sake, translated the three lines as one riddle; but line 3, taken on its own, is certainly self-contained.

Riddle 69. Though *singeð þurh sidan* seems to indicate a wind instrument, Dobbie notes that 'the description in lines 2b–4a seems to favour "harp".' However, a shepherd's pipe is more likely to have been hung up by the wayside than a harp. Cf. Virg. *Ecl.* vii, 24.

Riddle 73. The new solution, Snow, is proposed by A. R. V. Cooper in *Agenda* vol. 19, no. 1. 'A singular man' is masculine singular, a grammatical description of the word for snow in Old English.

Riddle 75. Possibly a false start to a riddle, possibly to be solved as 'hen', as Mackie suggests.

Riddle 79. Line 6 is a reference to the honey in the mead. Horn was used for many purposes in Anglo-Saxon times.

Riddle 80. The last line and a half are damaged by fire. I have translated Holthausen's *ond ic þæt þolian sceal/forþon ic wrecan ne mæg wonsceaft mine*; this was before I read Dobbie's observation that this emendation was too long. However, Dobbie's own *ne ic wepan mæg* could just as easily read *wrecan*.

Riddle 85. The solution proposed borrows (like the riddle itself) from Symphosius' Riddle 95, *luscus allium vendens*.

THE DREAM OF THE ROOD (p. 83)

I have used throughout the text of Bruce Dickins and A. S. C. Ross in their handy edition in Methuen's Old English Library. The text also appears in Sweet's *Reader*. Aspects of the poem not fully covered in the Methuen edition are dealt with in articles by Patch (*Liturgical Influence in The Dream of the Rood*, PMLA xxiv, pp. 233–57) and Woolf (*Doctrinal Influences in the Dream of the Rood*, Medium Aevum, vol. 27, no. 3, 1958). The comprehensive edition by Michael Swanton (Manchester University Press, 1970) supersedes Dickins and Ross; its introduction is especially useful on the cult of the Cross from Constantine's original vision onwards.

l. 8. I interpret with Sweet, though Patch's suggestion (that *foldan sceatum* means the corners of the earth, and that the Rood is here thought of as reaching out to them) is attractive. *Eorðan sceatas* in line 37 obviously refers to the earth's surface.

l. 8. Five jewels: Patch mentions the occurrence of crosses with five jewels in early mosaics. The five grains of incense, symbolic of the five wounds, placed in the Paschal Candle might also have suggested this.

l. 13. *sigebeam*: Patch quotes several references from the Liturgy to the *lignum triumphale*, for example the famous hymn *Vexilla regis prodeunt*. Woolf notes that Christ is presented in this poem as *Christus miles*, the champion who conquers death. It is only in the later Middle Ages that the suffering and pathos of the Crucifixion are emphasized more than this heroic aspect.

l. 15. *wædum geweorðod*: I have taken this as parallel to *gegyred mid golde*. *Wædum* (weeds) usually means 'clothing', but Bosworth-Toller seems to allow this meaning.

l. 19. *earmra*: cf. *fracodes* in line 10.

l. 22. Patch's explanation is plausible: the alternation of gold and blood is related to the two natures in the single person of Christ (the human, which is passible, the divine, which is not) – reflected in the change of colour of the vestments on Palm Sunday, when the red cross of Lent gives way to a more ornamental cross.

l. 26. *þæt*: 'how', as Sweet notes.

l. 36. Dickins and Ross note that this echoes Matthew 27, verse 51: *terra mota est et petrae scissae sunt*.

l. 39. *hæleð*, hero: The assimilation of the New Testament story into Germanic terms is complete. In line 42 and elsewhere the Cross refuses to disobey its lord.

ll. 55–6. 'All creation wept.' Dickins and Ross cite the striking parallel of all creation weeping to rescue Baldr from Hel in the Norse Prose Eddas.

l. 63. Woolf notes that it is nowhere said that Christ actually died.

l. 76. Referring to the Invention of the Cross by the Empress Helena, Constantine's mother.

BRUNANBURH (p. 95)

The edition followed is that of John C. Pope in *Seven Old English Poems* (1981).

l. 1. Athelstan: King of Wessex, Mercia and England, 924–39.

l. 3. Edmund: Ironside, aged 16 at the time of the battle, King 939–46.

l. 6. 'lindens': limewood shields.
'leavings of hammers': swords.

l. 7. Edward: the Elder, Alfred's eldest son, King 899–924.

l. 11. 'shipmen': Vikings.

l. 18. 'Northerners': Vikings.

l. 26. Anlaf: Olaf Guthfrithson of Dublin.

l. 28. 'five kings': other annals confirm this.

l. 30. 'earls': Norse *jarls*.

l. 32. 'scant': that is, no.

l. 33. 'prince': Anlaf.

l. 36. 'slipped away': that is, disgracefully.

l. 37. 'The old king': Constantine III of Scots.

l. 44. 'yield': that is, the slaughter.

l. 45. 'chieftain': Constantine.

l. 55. 'Dingsmere': the Irish Sea.

l. 70. 'since': that is, since the fifth century.

THE BATTLE OF MALDON (p. 99)

I have used E. V. Gordon's edition in Methuen's Old English Library, now revised by Scragg and published by Manchester U.P. The text is also to be found in Sweet. E. D. Laborde's article in the *English Historical Review* xl, pp. 161 ff. (1925) successfully identified the site of the battle, but all the information necessary for the full appreciation of the poem is in Gordon's edition.

l. 2. 'He' is Bryhtnoth. Fighting was done on foot, and the sending away of the horses shows that there was no intention of retreat.

l. 5. Offa seems to have been Bryhtnoth's second-in-command, and leads the English after the Earl's death.

l. 6. *se eorl:* Bryhtnoth. *eorl* is derived from Scandinavian *jarl*, and is here used in its fullest sense of Ealdorman, or ruler of the East Saxons. Elsewhere, of course, 'an earl' is merely synonymous for 'a warrior'. Bryhtnoth was one of the most powerful Ealdormen of his day, both in lands and in personal influence, and is historically important as one of the most vigorous supporters of the reform of the monasteries and the friend of three successive kings. The historian of the monastery of Ely, to which Bryhtnoth gave much land, records in the twelfth century that 'He was eloquent, robust, of great bodily stature . . . and remarkably brave and free from the fear of death'. He seems to have made a great impression on his age. All the other evidence corroborates the picture given of him in the poem – that he was pious, impetuous, an experienced war-leader, and that his hair was 'swan-white'. E. V. Gordon, from whose introduction this information is taken, has calculated that at the time of the battle he would have been sixty-five or more. I reproduce an account he cites of the investigation of Bryhtnoth's tomb in Ely Cathedral, where his remains had been transferred from Ely Abbey at the time of the Ely historian. This history relates that the Abbot and monks of Ely carried Bryhtnoth's body from the field after the battle, but that his head had been cut off and taken away by the Vikings. A letter read before the Society of Antiquaries in 1772 confirms this story, and also the tradition that he was of a gigantic height:

> I apprised those who attended on that occasion, 18 May 1769, that if my surmises were well-founded no head would be found in the cell which contained the Bones of Brithnoth, Duke of Northumberland . . . (Under the effigy of) Duke Brithnoth there were no remains of the head, though we searched diligently, and found most, if not all his other bones almost entire, and those remarkable for their length, and proportionally strong; which also agrees with what is recorded by the same historian with regard to the Duke's person, viz. that he was *viribus robustus, corpore maximus* . . . It was estimated . . . that the Duke must have been 6 feet 9 inches in stature. It was observed that the collar-bone had been nearly cut through, as by a battle-axe or two-handed sword.

l. 24. *heorðwerod:* This is the *comitatus* of Tacitus; 'not chance or the accident of mustering makes the troop or wedge, but family and friendship, and this is a very powerful incitement to valour.' *Germania*, 7, Mattingly's translation. The *heorðwerod* are distinguished from the *fyrd*, or local levy, who have to be taught how to stand.

l. 29. The Viking spokesman addresses his words both to 'thee' and 'you'. As E. V. Gordon says, 'there seems to be no difficulty in taking the sg. as applying specifically to Bryhtnoth and the pl. to the English generally'.

l. 42. The raising of the shield was to call for silence. There is no reason to suppose that the poetic convention does not mirror an actual convention of battle.

l. 51. *unforcuð:* 'not the meanest'. This is not the literal meaning; but litotes is a common trick in Old English verse.

l. 66. *lucon lagustreamas:* 'the sea's arms locked' – a description, as Laborde suggests, of the tide joining around the western end of Northey Island; this could have been seen by both sides quite clearly.

l. 75. Wulfstan may have been specially chosen to defend the *brycg* because the battle was being fought on his land. His son Leofwine leaves the land of Purleigh near the site of the battle, in his will, and Domesday makes no mention of land between Purleigh and the estuary, so we can even say this supposition is probable.

l. 77. *francan:* Frankish spears were esteemed; but, as E. V. Gordon shows, the word has lost any very precise denotation, being used interchangeably with *gar.* Here Wulfstan throws it; but in line 140 Bryhtnoth clearly thrusts it into his man.

l. 91. *ceallian ofer cald wæter:* cold is always baleful. All the destructive runes are connected with winter.

l. 98. 'sheer'. I have merely modernized the spelling of *scir,* in the hope that the ghost of the proper meaning – 'shining' – might still lurk in the word.

l. 102. 'war-hedge': the men in the second rank held their shields over their heads to protect the men in front as well as themselves. Ideally the shields overlapped, so that there would be no chink.

l. 106. Ravens occur in *Finnsburh,* 34 (translated, I fear, into crows), and in most Northern poems before battles.

l. 115. *swustersunu:* cf. *Widsith,* 45 n.; also *Germania,* 20.

l. 134. *superne:* cf. *francan,* line 77.

l. 160. *gefecgan:* cf. *Waldere* II, 16.

l. 169. *har hilderinc: cigneam canitiem sui capitis* of the *Vita Oswaldi.*

l. 181. 'heathen churls'; the opprobrium lay in the adjective.

l. 207. *oðer twega:* cf. *Waldere* I, 9.

l. 217. Aelfwine is with Bryhtnoth, as Gordon says, because he has been expelled from his patrimony. *Germania,* 14: 'Many noble youths, if the land of their birth is stagnating in a protracted peace, deliberately seek out other tribes, where some war is afoot.' This would apply to Beowulf's setting out for Denmark better than to the present passage, however.

l. 251. 'lordless'. Tacitus: 'Men have often survived battle only to end their shame by hanging themselves.' *Germania*, 6.

l. 255. Dunnere's speech is very short, which is perhaps fitting for a yeoman among the household companions. However, Leofsunu, who speaks for longer, does not seem to be of noble birth, so no rigid system of decorum can be said to overlay these actualities.

l. 265. The hostage is traditionally more loyal even than the lord's own retainers; cf. the hostages Walter and Hagen in *Waldere*, or the hostage in the story of Cynewulf and Cyneheard in the Chronicle.

l. 266. Bryhtnoth is described in the *Liber Eliensis* as *Northanimbrorum dux*, and he may have had some connection with Northumbria (as well as Mercia; see note above), though exactly what this may have been we do not know. See l. 6 n.

l. 300. I agree with Gordon, that *Wigelmes bearn* must refer to Offa, and have substituted his name for clarity's sake.

l. 309. Bryhtwold may not be the trusty old fellow of legend. See the Glossary of Proper Names.

APPENDIX A: THE RUNES

———— z ————

THE runic alphabet or *futhark* first came into being towards the end of the third century before Christ among the tribes of the South Tirol, who combined their Italic script with various magic symbols or pictographs commonly in use among the Germanic peoples: these earlier symbols had been used for sortilege, or the casting of lots, a practice to which the Germans were addicted, according to Tacitus (*Germania*, 10; also *Beowulf*, l. 204). Runic inscriptions are found on weapons, coins and such objects as the Franks Casket throughout Europe north of the Alps, and although they were adopted for Christian purposes (as, for example, on the Ruthwell Cross) the runes retain an unmistakably pagan character, even in England. The Synod of Clofesho (747) still found it necessary to condemn divination.

Runes never became completely secularized, as they were originally conceived as signs to be carved, and never developed a cursive form. They were used for secret writing and for riddling; Cynewulf signs his poems with runes, as did the sender of *The Husband's Message*. One or two runes were adopted for the Anglo-Saxon alphabet – þ for example, which is the sign at once for Thorn (which it resembles visually) and for the 'th' sound. This has survived into our own day as the 'Y' of Ye Olde Tea Shoppe. It is a characteristic irony that þ was, according to Elliott's *Runes*, the rune associated with the Gothic *thurisaz*, a demon, before it was given its more innocuous meaning of Thorn. For further information on the subject R. W. V. Elliott's *Runes. An Introduction* (1959, rev. 1989) should be consulted.

The Husband's Message ends:

> Gecyre ic ætsomme · ᚻ · ᚱ · geador
> · ᛦ · ᚹ · *ond* · ᛗ · aþe benemnan.
> þæt he þa wære · *ond* þa wintetreowe
> be him lifgendum · læstan wolde
> þe git on ærdagum · oft gespræcon

As Dobbie says, the punctuation of the runes in the MS. indicates that they are to be read separately rather than in a group or groups; he proposes two solutions in his Notes. Elliott has given what seems to me a more convincing interpretation. Taking the last rune as the M-rune rather than the D-rune, he gives the message (somewhat expanded) as: 'Follow the *sun's path* (*sigel-rad*) south across the *ocean* (*ear*) to find *joy* (*wyn*) with the *man* (*mon*) who is waiting for you.' (*Runes*, p. 73).

The anagram runes in Riddle 42 are used simply as shorthand, their initial letters spelling out the solution. They are ᛏ, ᛝ, ᚱ and ᚻ; their meanings are given in my translation.

APPENDIX B: SUGGESTED
SOLUTIONS TO THE RIDDLES

———z———

7 Swan
9 Cuckoo
12 Oxhide
25 Onion
26 Gospel Book
27 Mead
29 Moon and Sun
30 A Beam of Wood
33 Iceberg, Ice
34 Rake
35 Coat of Mail
38 Bullock
42 Cock and Hen
43 Soul and Body

44 Key
47 Bookworm
50 Fire
51 Handwriting
57 Jackdaws or Crows
60 Reed
68 Ice
69 Shepherd's Pipe
73 Snow
75 Mirror
76 Oyster
79 Horn
80 Weathercock
84 Fish in River
85 A One-eyed Garlic Seller

APPENDIX C: ANGLO-SAXON
METRIC

———————— z ————————

I HAVE outlined in the Introduction (pp. xvii ff.) the way in which the half-lines of Old English verse are bound together. Here I wish to list simply the five patterns into which the stresses usually fall. They were first 'discovered' by the nineteenth-century German scholar, Sievers, and they were undoubtedly adhered to by the old poets. By this I do not mean that there were academic rules for the construction of Old English verse; but the *scop* instinctively used the traditional measures of his craft.

A schematic presentation of the five basic half-lines may give a misleading impression of rigidity, especially as we are dealing with a stressed, not a quantitative, language. Even now every word in the English language is liable to be stressed, pitched, articulated and pronounced slightly differently according to context. Nevertheless, 'scansion' has its rule-of-thumb value when one is trying to break the code of a new rhythm. And Anglo-Saxon verse composition was an intricate and difficult art.

The best introduction to the metric is J. R. R. Tolkien's Prefatory Remarks to J. R. Clark Hall's translation of *Beowulf* (Allen & Unwin, 1941); the following schema is reproduced from there.

A	falling-falling	: *knights in | ármour.*
		4 1 4 1
B	rising-rising	: *the róar | ing séa.*
		1 4 1 4
C	clashing	: *on hígh | móuntains.*
		1 4 4 or 3 1
	a falling by stages	: *bríght | árchàngels.*
D	or	4 3 2 1
	b broken fall	: *bóld | brázenfàced.*
		4 3 1 2
E	fall and rise	: *híghcrésted | hélms*
		4 2 1 4 or 3

A, B, C have equal feet, each containing a lift and dip. D and
E have unequal feet: one consists of a single lift, the other has
a subordinate stress (marked ̀) inserted.

GLOSSARY OF PROPER NAMES

——————— z ———————

THIS glossary is intended to be complete; the only names I have not glossed are those of tribes or heroes in *Widsith* about which nothing certain is known and the names in the new translation of *Brunanburh* added in the third edition, which are glossed in the notes to that poem. Any other names occurring in the poems should be here.

AELFERE One of Wulfstan's companions at the *brycg*. *Maldon*, 80.

AELFHERE Father of Waldere. *Waldere* I, 11; II, 18.

AELFNOTH A follower of Bryhtnoth who stood at his side in the battle. *Maldon*, 183.

AELFRIC Father of Aelfwine. Ealdorman of Mercia in 893, banished two years later for political reasons, and on that account not mentioned by Aelfwine in boasting of his lineage. *Maldon*, 209.

AELFWINE Kinsman of Bryhtnoth, son of Aelfric and grandson to Ealhelm. *Maldon*, 211, 231.

AELFWINE The name given to Alboin, leader of Lombard invasion of Italy in 568 and the last of the Germanic conquerors of Rome. *Widsith*, 70 ff.

AETHELGAR Father of the Godric who did not flee at Maldon. *Maldon*, 320.

AETHELRED King of England 978–1016. He was the second King Aethelred. The literal meaning of the two components of his name – *æthel-ræd* – is 'noble and resourceful', but because of his repeated failure to withstand the Danish invasions he was known as *Æthelræd-unræd*. Hence the modern 'the Unready'. *Maldon*, 53, 151, 203.

AETHERIC One of Bryhtnoth's retainers, possibly the Aetheric who was later suspected of plotting to recognize Sweyn, the Viking, as king of Essex. Brother of Sibyrht. *Maldon*, 280.

ALEXANDREAS Alexander the Great. Famous in heroic times, he later became the hero of cycles of romance. His mention at *Widsith*, 15, is not necessarily an interpolation.

ANGEL The continental home of the Angles, to be located in Denmark and the Danish islands. *Widsith*, 35, 61.

ASHFERTH Son of Edgeleave; a Northumbrian hostage of noble birth who fights bravely for Bryhtnoth. *Maldon*, 267.

ATTILA King of the Huns, conqueror of Rome, d. 453. Though not a German, celebrated in Germanic tradition in the company of Eormanric and Alboin. *Widsith*, 18, *Waldere* 1, 6.

BEADOHILD The Bothvildr of the *Völundarkviða*, Nithhad's daughter. Wayland killed her two brothers and ravished her before escaping from Nithhad. She is cited in the second strophe of *Deor* as an example of misfortune outlived because the son born of this union was Widia, who became a great hero.

BECCA One of Eormanric's followers, ruler of the Banings. In legend, the evil counsellor who advised Eormanric to murder Sunilda. *Widsith*, 115.

BEOWULF The protagonist of the poem. Son of Edgethew, nephew of the historical king of the Geats, Hygelac.

BRECA Ruler of the Brondings, as in *Beowulf*, where he has a five-day swimming match with the hero of the poem. *Widsith*, 25.

BRIGHTHELM Byrhtelm, father of Bryhtnoth. *Maldon*, 92.

BRYHTNOTH The English leader at Maldon, son of Byrhtelm. See Notes, p. 143. In the Anglo-Saxon his name is properly Byrhtnoth (battle-bright), but I have 'metathesized' the 'r' for euphony.

BURGUNDIANS An East Germanic tribe who later founded a kingdom in the Rhineland. Defeated by the opposition of Huns in the east and Gauls in the west. The central characters of some of the *Eddas*, the *Nibelungenlied* and Wagner's *Ring* come from the Burgundian royal house. Guthere is their leader. *Waldere* 11, 14; *Widsith*, 19, 65.

BYRHTWOLD The *eald geneat* of Bryhtnoth who speaks the famous lines beginning at *Maldon*, 213. Either a trusted retainer or (if he is identified with Brihtwold, *cniht* of Aethelflaed, Bryhtnoth's widow) a member of the Ealdorman's closest personal following.

CEOLA Father of Wulfstan. *Maldon*, 76.

DANES Originally (e.g. in *Widsith*, 35) inhabitants of southern Sweden. When the Angles invaded England, the Danes crossed into the country now called after them. Hrothgar's people – the tribe best known in Anglian tradition. Bryhtnoth's opponents at Maldon.

DUNNERE A simple churl who stands with the nobles of Bryhtnoth's household. *Maldon*, 255.

EADGILS Widsith's lord, chief of the Myrgings. *Widsith*, 93 n.

EADRIC One of Bryhtnoth's retainers. *Maldon*, 11.

EADWINE (EDWIN) Father of Aelfwine (Alboin) at *Widsith*, 74, and Ealhhild at *Widsith*, 99. King of the Lombards.

EADWOLD Retainer of Bryhtnoth, brother to Oswold. *Maldon*, 304.

EAHA One of Hnaef's followers at Finnsburg. *Finnsburg*, 15.

EALHELM Grandfather of Aelfwine, father-in-law of Aelfric Ealdorman of Mercia. Called *dux* on royal charters. *Maldon*, 218.

EALHHILD Daughter of Eadwine, king of the Lombards, wife of Eormanric the Goth. She gives Widsith a ring. Possibly to be identified with the Sunilda of Jordanes. See *Widsith*, 5 *n.*

EASTGOTA Ostrogotha, the founder of the Ostrogoths. Mentioned at *Widsith*, 113, as one of Eormanric's followers and the father of Unwen. He would have been Eormanric's great-great-grandfather.

EATS The Jutes, said by Bede to have come to Kent from Jutland, though scholars disagree. *Widsith*, 26.

EDGELEAVE Father of Ashferth. *Maldon*, 267.

EDGETHEW Beowulf's father.

EDWARD Bryhtnoth's bower-thane or chamberlain. *Maldon*, 117. The 'Long Edward' of line 273 may be the same person.

EMERCA *Widsith*, 113 *n.*

EORMANRIC The great king of the Ostrogoths, who in the third quarter of the fourth century ruled an empire that stretched from the Baltic to the Black Sea, according to Jordanes. Died 375. He was later credited with the murder of his son Frederick and his nephews the Herelings; also with the exiling of Dietrich von Bern. In legend he was a treacherous tyrant (*Widsith, Deor, Beowulf*). See *Widsith*, 9 *n.*

FIFELDOR An island at the mouth of the River Eider. See *Widsith*, 35 *n.*

FINN FOLCWALDING The lord of Finnsburg, leader of the Frisians (*Widsith*, 27); not actually mentioned in the *Finnsburg Fragment*. His name means Folk-ruler.

FINNSBURG Finn's stronghold, the scene of *The Fight at Finnsburg*. Its whereabouts in the Frisian islands are unknown. *Finnsburg*, 36.

FRANKS The Germanic founders of France. *Widsith*, 24, 68.

FRIDLA *Widsith*, 113 *n.*

FRISIANS The inhabitants of the marshes now drained to make the polders of Holland; Finn's people, *Widsith*, 27. Traditionally a seafaring race. *Gnomic Verses*, 95.

GADD A kinsman of Offa. *Maldon*, 287.

GARULF A young Frisian who falls at Finnsburg. Guthlaf's son. *Finnsburg*, 18, 31.

GEATS Beowulf's people. They inhabited the area south of the lakes Wener and Wetter in southern Sweden. *Widsith*, 58.

GIFECA Ruler of the Burgundians when they were neighbours of the Goths and Huns on the Vistula. *Widsith*, 19.

GISLHERE A Burgundian ancestor of Guthere mentioned at *Widsith*, 123, as one of the lords of Gothland.

GODRIC The loyal retainer of Bryhtnoth who fought till the end. Aethelgar's son. *Maldon*, 321.

GODRIC, GODWINE, and GODWIY The three sons of Odda who fled the battlefield. *Maldon*, 187, 192, 237, 325.

GRENDEL The monster who terrorizes Heorot, killed by Beowulf. A demon, sprung from the race of Cain.

GUTHERE Gundahari, king of the Burgundians, who died in 436 in a famous last stand against the Huns. In *Widsith* he is presented as a gold-giver (66 ff.). In *Waldere*, he and Hagen waylay the hero. *Waldere* I, 25. For his later fame, see *Widsith*, 65–7 n.

GUTHERE A Frisian who tries to restrain Garulf at Finnsburg. Possibly Garulf's uncle. *Finnsburg*, 18.

GUTHLAF A follower of Hnaef at Finnsburg. Sent by Hengest to gather help in Denmark. Possibly the Hunlafing of *Beowulf*. *Finnsburg*, 16.

GUTHLAF Father of Garulf. *Finnsburg*, 33.

HAGEN Guthere's champion; he is always found with his lord in Germanic tradition; probably a historical character. *Waldere* II, 15.

HAGEN Leader of the Holm-Riggs or Island-Rugians, a tribe who lived in the German Baltic islands. See *Widsith*, 21 n.

HAMA A famous outlaw, mentioned with Widia at *Widsith*, 124, among the heroes of Gothland.

HEATHOBARDS A tribe who had a blood-feud with the Danes, possibly to be identified with the Heruli. See *Widsith*, 49 n.

HENGEST Second-in-command of the Danes at Finnsburg, he succeeds Hnaef as leader. Possibly the Hengest who invaded Kent. *Finnsburg*, 17.

HEODEN Ruler of the Gloms, a tribe of the Baltic coast of Germany. *Widsith*, 21 n. Founder of the Heodenings, Deor's tribe.

HEODENINGS The word means children of Heoden. *Deor*, 36.

HEOROT Hrothgar's famous hall, the scene of the slaughter of the Heathobards. *Widsith*, 49. *Beowulf*, passim.

HEORRENDA Deor's successor as poet of the Heodenings. See also *Widsith*, 21 n.

HERELINGS Eormanric's nephews, Emerca and Fridla, supposed to have been murdered by him at Sifeca's instigation. *Widsith*, 112.

HILDEGUTH Betrothed to Waldere. She is not mentioned by name in the Fragments, but the first speech is obviously hers, and I have introduced her name into the text.

HNAEF Leader of the Danes at Finnsburg. He is called the son of Hoc in *Beowulf*, and at *Widsith*, 29, the ruler of the Hocingas. *Finnsburg*, 1, 40.

HOLM-RIGGS Island-Rugians. *Widsith*, 21 *n*.

HROTHGAR King of the Danes, uncle of Hrothwulf, builder of Heorot. See note on *Widsith*, 45 ff.

HROTHWULF, HROTHULF Hrothgar's nephew, the famous Hrolf Kraki of Norse tradition. See note on *Widsith*, 45 ff.

HUNLAFING See Guthlaf.

HWALA Sceaf's grandson, according to the genealogy of the West Saxon royal house given in three versions of the Anglo-Saxon Chronicle. *Widsith*, 14.

HYGELAC King of the Geats, Beowulf's uncle. Mentioned in Gregory of Tours's *Historia Francorum* as having died in a raid on the Frisians, who at that time (521) formed part of the Merovingian Empire. The only character in *Beowulf* who is quite certainly historical.

INGELD Chief of the Heathobards. *Widsith*, 48 *n*.

KAISER The Emperor, either of the East (*Widsith*, 76) or of the West (*Widsith*, 20).

LEOFSUNU One of Bryhtnoth's men, from Sturmer, Essex. *Maldon*, 244.

LOMBARDS In the second century a tribe living between the Angles and the Swaefe on the north German coast, ruled by Sheaf (*Widsith*, 32). Under Aelfwine (Alboin) they invaded Italy in the sixth century. Also at *Widsith*, 80.

MACCUS The third defender of the *brycg* (*Maldon*, 80). The name indicates Norse descent.

MIMMING Waldere's sword, made by Wayland and usually said to belong to his son, Widia. *Waldere* 1, 3.

MYRGINGS Widsith's people, identified in the poem with the Swaefe. They lived between the Eider and the Elbe.

NITHHAD Father of Beadohild, enslaver of Wayland, as related in the first strophe of *Deor*. Mentioned as Widia's grandfather in *Waldere* II, 8.

ODDA Father of Godric, Godwine, and Godwiy. *Maldon*, 186, 238.

OFFA I The fourth-century founder of the Angles. *Widsith*, 35 *n*.

OFFA II King of Mercia in the eighth century. Builder of the Welsh dyke.

OFFA Bryhtnoth's second-in-command, a kinsman of Gadd; he leads the English after his lord's death and the flight of Godric. *Maldon*, 5, 198, 230, 286, 288.

ONGENTHEOW King of the Swedes, often mentioned in *Beowulf*. *Widsith*, 31.

ORDLAF A Dane, follower of Hnaef at Finnsburg. See under Guthlaf. *Finnsburg*, 16.

OSWOLD Retainer of Bryhtnoth, brother of Eadwold. *Maldon*, 304.

PANT, PANTA The River Blackwater, which flows out to the sea below Maldon in Essex; still known by this name in the stretch below the town, according to E. Ekwall's *English River Names*.

ROME-WELSH Romans. 'Welsh' means 'foreign'. *Widsith*, 69, 78.

SAEFERTH See Sigeferth.

SAXONS The inhabitants of the German North Sea coast who invaded southern England. *Widsith*, 62.

SCEAF Ruler of the Lombards, *Widsith*, 32. Mythical civilizer of the tribes of the North Sea coast, his name signifies the introduction of tillage. He stands at the head of the West Saxon genealogies. Under the name of Scyld Shefing, he is also the founder of the Danes.

SCYLD Scyld Shefing, the founder of the Danish royal house; Hrothgar's great-grandfather. *Beowulf*, 26.

SCYLDINGS The children of Scyld; used of the Danes and of the Danish royal house.

SEAFOLA Mentioned with Theodoric as one of Eormanric's followers at *Widsith*, 115. The historical Sabene of Ravenna.

SECGAN Seggs. See under Sigeferth.

SERINGS (?) Syrians. *Widsith*, 75.

SHILLING Widsith's fellow-*scop*. *Widsith*, 103.

SIBYRHT Retainer of Bryhtnoth, brother of Aetheric. *Maldon*, 282.

SIFECA A follower of Eormanric; in legend, the traitor who prompted Eormanric's murder of the Herelings. *Widsith*, 116.

SIGEFERTH One of Hnaef's followers at Finnsburg, identical with the Saeferth who rules the Seggs at *Widsith*, 31.

SIGEMUND The great dragon-slayer. See *Beowulf*, 875 *n*.

SLIDING-FINNS A tribe who used snowshoes, probably Lapps. *Widsith*, 79.

SWAEFE Suevi, but not to be identified with the famous southern branch. See under Myrgings. *Widsith*, 22, 44, 61.

SWEDES A tribe who inhabited only a small part of southern Sweden. *Widsith*, 31, 58.

THEODRIC Theodoric the Frank (*Widsith*, 24). The eldest son of

Clovis, and himself king at Rheims from 511 to 534.

THEODRIC Theodoric the Ostrogoth, mentioned as one of Eormanric's retainers at *Widsith*, 115. Leader of the Ostrogothic nation into Italy, where they overcame Odoacer's Germans. Theodoric killed Odoacer in his palace at Ravenna on 15 March, 493. He ruled from Verona for thirty years. In the *Nibelungenlied* he becomes the greatest knight, Dietrich von Bern. *Deor*, 18; *Waldere* II, 4.

THURSTAN Father of Wistan. *Maldon*, 298.

VENDELS The inhabitants of modern Vendsyssel in Jutland; not the Vandals. *Widsith*, 59.

VIKINGS A general name for sea raiders; possibly a proper name at *Widsith*, 59.

WADE Ruler of the Haelsings. Originally a sea-giant. See *Widsith*, 22 n.

WALDERE Walter of Aquitaine. In *Waltharius* the son of Alphere of Aquitaine, but *Waldere* itself gives no clues as to his identity or origin.

WAYLAND The Smith of Germanic legend. See *Deor*, 1 n.; *Waldere* II, 9.

WIDIA The early Gothic champion Vidigioia, mentioned by the Latin historian Jordanes. In the lays he becomes the son of Wayland and Beadohild, and directly associated with Theodoric. At *Widsith*, 124 and 130, he and Hama are mentioned as the exiles who rule one of the peoples of Gothland. *Waldere* II, 4, 9.

WIDSITH The wandering poet of *Widsith*. Represented as a Myrging.

WIGELM Father of Offa. See *Maldon*, 300 n.

WISTAN Son of Thurstan, retainer of Bryhtnoth. *Maldon*, 297.

WULFMAER Son of Bryhtnoth's sister. *Maldon*, 113.

WULFMAER *SE GEONGA* The boy who stood at Bryhtnoth's side, not the same person as the above. *Maldon*, 155, 183.

WULFSTAN Son of Ceola, father of Wulfmaer *se geonga*. The Horatius of the *brycg* (*Maldon*, 75, 79, 155). The battle may have been fought on his land. See 75 n.

FURTHER READING

———— z ————

GENERAL

Bruce Mitchell and Fred C. Robinson, *A Guide to Old English*, 4th ed. (Oxford: Basil Blackwell, 1988), an introduction to the language with extracts and a good annotated bibliography. Also recommended are: Stanley B. Greenfield and Daniel G. Calder, *A New Critical History of Old English Literature* (New York University Press; University of London Press, 1986); Barbara C. Raw, *The Art and Background of Old English Poetry* (London: Edward Arnold, 1978); T. A. Shippey, *Old English Verse* (London: Hutchinson, 1972); and C. L. Wrenn, *A Study of Old English Literature* (London: Harrap, 1967). James Campbell (editor), *The Anglo-Saxons* (Oxford: Phaidon, 1982) is the best single introduction.

Allen, Michael J. B., and Calder, Daniel G.: *Sources and Analogues of Old English Poetry: The Major Latin Texts in Translation* (Cambridge: D. S. Brewer; Totowa, New Jersey; Rowman & Littlefield, 1976).

Bede: *A History of the English Church and People*, edited and translated by Leo Sherley-Price, revised by R. E. Latham (Harmondsworth: Penguin, 1968).

Brown, Peter: *The World of Late Antiquity* (London: Thames & Hudson, 1971).

Bruce-Mitford, Rupert: *The Sutton Hoo Ship Burial*, 3 vols. (London: British Museum, 1983).

Chadwick, H. M., and Chadwick, Nora K.: *The Ancient Literature of Europe*, vol. 1 of *The Growth of Literature* (Cambridge University Press, 1932).

Finberg, H. P. R.: *The Formation of England 550–1042* (London: Hart-Davis, MacGibbon, 1974; Paladin, 1976).

Ford, B. (editor): *The Cambridge Guide to the Arts in Britain*, vol. 1. (Cambridge: Cambridge U.P., 1988).

Henderson, George: *Early Mediaeval* (Harmondsworth: Penguin, 1972).

Ker, W. P.: *The Dark Ages* (London, 1904; Hyperion, Connecticut, 1979); *Epic and Romance* (London, 1896; New York: Dover, 1957).

Lord, Albert B.: *The Singer of Tales* (New York: Atheneum, 1965).

Nordenfalk, Carl: *Celtic and Anglo-Saxon Painting* (London: Chatto & Windus, 1977).

Page, R. I.: *Life in Anglo-Saxon England* (London: Batsford, 1970).

Stenton, Sir Frank: *Anglo-Saxon England*, 3rd ed. (Oxford: Clarendon Press, 1971).

Tacitus, Publius Cornelius: *Germania*, translated by H. S. Mattingly in *Tacitus on Britain and Germany* (Harmondsworth: Penguin, 1950).

Whitelock, Dorothy: *The Beginnings of English Society* (Harmondsworth: Penguin, 1960).

Wilson, David M.: *The Anglo-Saxons*, revised edition (Harmondsworth: Penguin, 1971).

LANGUAGE

Davis, Norman: *Sweet's Anglo-Saxon Primer* (Oxford: Clarendon Press, 1953).

Quirk, Randolph, and Wrenn, C. L.: *An Old English Grammar* (London; Methuen, 1955).

EDITIONS

Alexander, M., and Riddy, F. J. (editors): *The Macmillan Anthology of English Literature*, vol. 1, *The Middle Ages* (London, 1989).

Klaeber, Friedrich (editor): *Beowulf*, 3rd edn. (Boston: D. C. Heath, 1950).

Krapp, G. P., and Dobbie, E. V. K.: *The Anglo-Saxon Poetic Records*, 6 vols. (New York: Columbia University Press; London: Routledge, 1931–54).

Pope, John C.: *Seven Old English Poems*, 2nd edn. (New York: Norton, 1981).

Scragg, D. G. (editor): *The Battle of Maldon* (Manchester: Manchester U.P., 1981).

Swanton, M. (editor): *The Dream of the Rood* (Manchester: Manchester U.P., 1970).

Whitelock, Dorothy: *Sweet's Anglo-Saxon Reader* (Oxford: Clarendon Press, 1970).

Wrenn, C. L. (editor): *Beowulf*, 3rd edn rev. Bolton (London: Harrap, 1973).

LITERARY HISTORY AND CRITICISM

Alexander, Michael: *History of Old English Literature* (London: Macmillan; New York: Schocken, 1983).

Nicholson, Lewis (editor): *An Anthology of Beowulf Criticism* (Notre Dame, Indiana: University of Indiana Press, 1963).

Opland, Jeff: *Anglo-Saxon Oral Poetry: A Study of the Traditions* (New Haven and London, 1980).

Stanley, E. G. (editor): *Continuations and Beginnings* (London: Nelson, 1966).

Tolkien, J. R. R.: 'Beowulf, the Monsters and the Critics', in *Proceedings of the British Academy*, XXII (London: Oxford University Press, 1936); also in Nicholson, *An Anthology*.

TRANSLATIONS

Alexander, Michael: *Old English Riddles from the Exeter Book* (London: Anvil Press Poetry, 1980, 1984).

The Anglo-Saxon Chronicle, G. N. Garmonsway (London: Dent, 1953; New York: Dutton, 1954).

The Anglo-Saxon Chronicle, a revised translation, edited by Dorothy Whitelock with David C. Douglas and Susie I. Tucker (London: Eyre and Spottiswoode, 1961).

Beowulf, Michael Alexander (Harmondsworth: Penguin, 1973).

Beowulf and its Analogues, G. N. Garmonsway and J. Simpson (London: Dent; New York: Dutton, 1968).

Bradley, S. A. J.: *Anglo-Saxon Poetry*, (London: Dent, 1982).

Swanton, Michael: *Anglo-Saxon Prose* (London: Dent; Totawa, New Jersey: Rowman and Littlefield, 1975).

Whitelock, Dorothy: *English Historical Documents*, vol. 1: *500–1042*, 2nd edn (London: Eyre Methuen, 1972).

Penguin Classics

LEGENDS FROM THE ANCIENT NORTH

BEOWULF

THE ELDER EDDA

THE SAGA OF THE VOLSUNGS

SIR GAWAIN AND THE GREEN KNIGHT

THE WANDERER: ELEGIES, EPICS, RIDDLES

J. R. R. Tolkien spent much of his life studying, translating and teaching the great epic stories of northern Europe, filled with heroes, dragons, trolls, dwarves and magic. He was hugely influential for his advocacy of *Beowulf* as a great work of literature and, even if he had never written *The Hobbit* and *The Lord of the Rings*, would be recognised today as a significant figure in the rediscovery of these extraordinary tales.

Legends from the Ancient North brings together from Penguin Classics five of the key works behind Tolkien's fiction. They are startling, brutal, strange pieces of writing, with an elemental power brilliantly preserved in these translations. They plunge the reader into a world of treachery, quests, chivalry, trials of strength. They are the most ancient narratives that exist from northern Europe and bring us as near as we will ever get to the origins of the magical landscape of Middle-earth (Midgard) which Tolkien remade in the 20th century.

PENGUIN CLASSICS

THE PROSE EDDA
SNORRI STURLSON

'What was the beginning, or how did things start? What was there before?'

The Prose Edda is the most renowned of all works of Scandinavian literature and our most extensive source for Norse mythology. Written in Iceland a century after the close of the Viking Age, it tells ancient stories of the Norse creation epic and recounts the battles that follow as gods, giants, dwarves and elves struggle for survival. It also preserves the oral memory of heroes, warrior kings and queens. In clear prose interspersed with powerful verse, the *Edda* provides unparalleled insight into the gods' tragic realization that the future holds one final cataclysmic battle, Ragnarok, when the world will be destroyed. These tales from the pagan era have proved to be among the most influential of all myths and legends, inspiring modern works as diverse as Wagner's *Ring* cycle and Tolkien's *The Lord of the Rings*.

This new translation by Jesse Byock captures the strength and subtlety of the original, while his introduction sets the tales fully in the context of Norse mythology. This edition includes also detailed notes and appendices.

Translated with an introduction, glossary and notes by Jesse Byock

PENGUIN CLASSICS

THE RUBA'IYAT OF OMAR KHAYYAM

'Many like you come and many go
Snatch your share before you are snatched away'

Revered in eleventh-century Persia as an astronomer, mathematician and philosopher, Omar Khayyam is now known first and foremost for his *Ruba'iyat*. The short epigrammatic stanza form allowed poets of his day to express personal feelings, beliefs and doubts with wit and clarity, and Khayyam became one of its most accomplished masters with his touching meditations on the transience of human life and of the natural world. One of the supreme achievements of medieval literature, the reckless romanticism and the pragmatic fatalism in the face of death means these verses continue to hold the imagination of modern readers.

In this translation, Persian scholar Peter Avery and the poet John Heath-Stubbs have collaborated to recapture the sceptical, unorthodox spirit of the original by providing a near literal English version of the original verse. This edition also includes a map, appendices, bibliography and an introduction examining the *ruba'i* form and Khayyam's life and times.

'[Has] restored to that masterpiece all the fun, dash and vivacity' Jan Morris

Translated by Peter Avery and John Heath-Stubbs

PENGUIN CLASSICS

EGIL'S SAGA

'The sea-goddess has ruffled me,
stripped me bare of my loved ones'

Egil's Saga tells the story of the long and brutal life of the tenth-century warrior-poet and farmer Egil Skallagrimsson: a psychologically ambiguous character who was at once the composer of intricately beautiful poetry and a physical grotesque capable of staggering brutality. This Icelandic saga recounts Egil's progression from youthful savagery to mature wisdom as he struggles to defend his honour in a running feud against the Norwegian King Erik Blood-axe, fights for the English King Athelstan in his battles against Scotland and embarks on colourful Viking raids across Europe. Exploring issues as diverse as the question of loyalty, the power of poetry and the relationship between two brothers who love the same woman, *Egil's Saga* is a fascinating depiction of a deeply human character, and one of the true masterpieces of medieval literature.

This new translation by Bernard Scudder fully conveys the poetic style of the original. It also contains a new introduction by Svanhildur Óskarsdóttir, placing the saga in historical context, a detailed chronology, a chart of Egil's ancestors and family, maps and notes.

Translated by Bernard Scudder

Edited by Ornulfur Thorsson

Penguin Classics

THE SAGA OF GRETTIR THE STRONG

'The most valiant man who has ever lived in Iceland'

Composed at the end of the fourteenth century by an unknown author, *The Saga of Grettir the Strong* is one of the last great Icelandic sagas. It relates the tale of Grettir, an eleventh-century warrior struggling to hold on to the values of a heroic age as they are eclipsed by Christianity and a more pastoral lifestyle. Unable to settle into a community of farmers, Grettir becomes the aggressive scourge of both honest men and evil monsters – until, following a battle with the sinister ghost Glam, he is cursed to endure a life of tortured loneliness away from civilization, fighting giants, trolls and berserks. A mesmerizing combination of pagan ideals and Christian faith, this is a profoundly moving conclusion to the Golden Age of saga writing.

This is an updated edition of Bernard Scudder's acclaimed translation. The new introduction by Örnólfur Thorsson considers the influence of Christianity on Icelandic saga writing, and this edition also includes genealogical tables and a note on the translation.

Translated by Bernard Scudder

Edited with an introduction by Örnólfur Thorsson

PENGUIN CLASSICS

THE ODYSSEY
HOMER

'I long to reach my home and see the day of my return. It is my never-failing wish'

The epic tale of Odysseus and his ten-year journey home after the Trojan War forms one of the earliest and greatest works of Western literature. Confronted by natural and supernatural threats – shipwrecks, battles, monsters and the implacable enmity of the sea-god Poseidon – Odysseus must test his bravery and native cunning to the full if he is to reach his homeland safely and overcome the obstacles that, even there, await him.

E. V. Rieu's translation of *The Odyssey* was the very first Penguin Classic to be published, and has itself achieved classic status. For this edition, his text has been sensitively revised and a new introduction added to complement E. V. Rieu's original introduction.

'One of the world's most vital tales. *The Odyssey* remains central to literature'
Malcolm Bradbury.

Translated by E. V. Rieu
Revised translation by D. C. H. Rieu, with an introduction by Peter Jones

PENGUIN CLASSICS

THE ILIAD
HOMER

> 'Look at me. I am the son of a great man. A goddess was my mother.
> Yet death and inexorable destiny are waiting for me'

One of the foremost achievements in Western literature, Homer's *Iliad* tells the story of the darkest episode in the Trojan War. At its centre is Achilles, the greatest warrior-champion of the Greeks, and his refusal to fight after being humiliated by his leader Agamemnon. But when the Trojan Hector kills Achilles' close friend Patroclus, he storms back into battle to take revenge – although knowing this will ensure his own early death. Interwoven with this tragic sequence of events are powerfully moving descriptions of the ebb and flow of battle, of the domestic world inside Troy's besieged city of Ilium, and of the conflicts between the gods on Olympus as they argue over the fate of mortals.

E. V. Rieu's acclaimed translation of Homer's *Iliad* was one of the first titles published in Penguin Classics, and now has classic status itself. For this edition, Rieu's text has been revised, and a new introduction and notes by Peter Jones complement the original introduction.

Translated by E. V. Rieu

Revised and updated by Peter Jones with D. C. H. Rieu

Edited with an introduction and notes by Peter Jones

PENGUIN CLASSICS

JUST SO STORIES
RUDYARD KIPLING

'The rhinoceros took off his skin and carried it over his shoulder as he came down to the beach to bathe'

The Camel gets his Hump, the Whale his Throat and the Leopard his Spots in these bewitching stories which conjure up distant lands, the beautiful gardens of splendid palaces, the sea, the deserts, the jungle and its creatures. Inspired by Kipling's delight in human eccentricities and the animal world, and based on bedtime stories he told to his daughter, these strikingly imaginative fables explore the myths of creation, the nature of beasts and the origins of language and writing. They are linked by poems and scattered with Kipling's illustrations, which contain hidden jokes, symbols and puzzles. Among Kipling's most loved works, the *Just So Stories* have been continually in print since 1902.

Part of a series of new editions of Kipling's works in Penguin Classics, this volume contains a General Preface by Jan Montefiore and an introduction by Judith Plotz exploring the origins of the stories in Kipling's own life and in folklore, their place in classic children's literature and their extraordinary language.

Edited with an introduction by Judith Plotz
Series Editor Jan Montefiore

PENGUIN CLASSICS

THE MAN WHO WOULD BE KING: SELECTED STORIES
RUDYARD KIPLING

'They tell me that one never sees a dead person's face in a dream. Is that true?'

Rudyard Kipling is one of the most magical storytellers in the English language. This new selection brings together the best of his short writings, following the development of his work over fifty years. They take us from the harsh, cruel, vividly realized world of the 'Indian' stories that made his name, through the experimental modernism of his middle period to the highly-wrought subtleties of his later pieces. Including the tale of insanity and empire, 'The Man Who Would Be King', the high-spirited 'The Village that Voted the Earth Was Flat', the fable of childhood cruelty and revenge 'Baa Baa, Black Sheep', the menacing psychological study 'Mary Postgate' and the ambiguous portrayal of grief and mourning in 'The Gardener', here are stories of criminals, ghosts, femmes fatales, madness and murder.

Part of a series of new editions of Kipling's works in Penguin Classics, this volume contains a General Preface by Jan Montefiore and an introduction discussing Kipling's reputation and influence, the ambivalence of his writing and the fascination with 'otherness' expressed in his short works.

Edited with an introduction by Jan Montefiore
Series Editor Jan Montefiore

PENGUIN CLASSICS

THE EPIC OF GILGAMESH

> 'Surpassing all other kings, heroic in stature,
> brave scion of Uruk, wild bull on the rampage!
> Gilgamesh the tall, magnificent and terrible'

Miraculously preserved on clay tablets dating back as much as four thousand years, the poem of Gilgamesh, king of Uruk, is the world's oldest epic, predating Homer by many centuries. The story tells of Gilgamesh's adventures with the wild man Enkidu, and of his arduous journey to the ends of the earth in quest of the Babylonian Noah and the secret of immortality. Alongside its themes of family, friendship and the duties of kings, *The Epic of Gilgamesh* is, above all, about mankind's eternal struggle with the fear of death.

The Babylonian version has been known for over a century, but linguists are still deciphering new fragments in Akkadian and Sumerian. Andrew George's gripping translation brilliantly combines these into a fluent narrative and will long rank as the definitive English *Gilgamesh*.

'A masterly new verse translation' *The Times*

Translated with an introduction by Andrew George

PENGUIN CLASSICS

THE DEATH OF KING ARTHUR

'Lancelot has brought me such great shame as to dishonour me through my wife,
I shall never rest till they are caught together'

Recounting the final days of Arthur, this thirteenth-century French version of
the Camelot legend, written by an unknown author, is set in a world of fading
chivalric glory. It depicts the Round Table diminished in strength after the Quest
for the Holy Grail, and with its integrity threatened by the weakness of Arthur's
own knights. Whispers of Queen Guinevere's infidelity with his beloved comrade-
at-arms Sir Lancelot profoundly distress the trusting King, leaving him no match
for the machinations of the treacherous Sir Mordred. The human tragedy of
The Death of King Arthur so impressed Malory that he built his own Arthurian
legend on this view of the court – a view that profoundly influenced the English
conception of the 'great' King.

James Cable's translation brilliantly captures all the narrative urgency and spare
immediacy of style. In his introduction, he examines characterization, narrative
style, authorship and the work's place among the different versions of the Arthur
myth.

Translated by James Cable

Penguin Classics

GISLI SURSSON'S SAGA *AND*
THE SAGA OF THE PEOPLE OF EYRI

> 'Fate must find someone to speak through.
> Whatever is meant to happen will happen'

Based on oral tales that originated from historical events in tenth-century Iceland, these two sagas follow the fate of a powerful Viking family across two generations, from its Norwegian ancestry through fierce battles to defend its honour. *Gisli Sursson's Saga* is a story of forbidden love and divided loyalties, in which the heroic Gisli vows to avenge the murder of his 'sworn brother' and sets in motion a chain of bloody events that culminate in tragedy. *The Saga of the People of Eyri* continues the story with Snorri, a cunning leader of the next generation, who uses his intellect to restore social order. Blending gripping narrative, humour, the supernatural and shrewd observation, these tales reveal the richness of the saga tradition and present a vivid record of a society moving from individualism to a Christian ethic of reconciliation and order.

These clear, contemporary translations are accompanied by an introduction giving historical and literary background to the sagas. This edition also includes appendices, maps, notes on the texts, a glossary and an index of characters.

Translated by Martin S. Regal and Judy Quinn
Edited with an introduction by Vésteinn Ólason

PENGUIN CLASSICS

PLAIN TALES FROM THE HILLS
RUDYARD KIPLING

'You are all liars, you English'

Plain Tales from the Hills, Rudyard Kipling's first collection of short stories, established his reputation and brought India to the British imagination. Including the stories 'Lispeth', 'Beyond the Pale' and 'In the Pride of His Youth', they tell of soldiers, wise children, exiles, forbidden romances and divided identities, creating a rich portrait of Anglo-Indian society. Originally published for a newspaper in Lahore when Kipling was a journalist, the tales were later revised by him to re-create as vividly as possible the sights and smells of India for readers at home. Far from being a celebration of empire, these stories explore the barriers between races, classes and sexes, and convey all the tensions and contradictions of colonial life.

Part of a series of new editions of Kipling's works in Penguin Classics, this volume contains a General Preface by Jan Montefiore and an introduction by Kaori Nagai discussing Kipling's portrayal of the relationship between India and England, the role of the narrator in his *Plain Tales*, and the revisions that he made to them.

Edited with an introduction by Kaori Nagai
Series Editor Jan Montefiore